Personality Revolution

Innovative Approaches for Men and Women to Stand Out

Honey Horton

1

Personality Revolution

Table of Contents

Chapter 1: Introduction to Personality Revolution

Understanding the Concept of Personality

Personality is a multifaceted construct that has intrigued scholars, philosophers, and laypeople alike for centuries. It is the unique blend of characteristics, traits, and behaviors that define an individual and distinguish them from others. Understanding the concept of personality requires delving into the intricate interplay of biological, psychological, and social factors that shape who we are. This exploration is not merely an academic exercise; it is a journey into the essence of human nature and the forces that drive our actions, thoughts, and emotions.

At its core, personality is about individuality. It encompasses the enduring patterns of thoughts, feelings, and behaviors that make each person unique. These patterns are influenced by a combination of genetic predispositions and environmental experiences. The debate over the relative contributions of nature and nurture to personality development has been a central theme in psychology. While genetic factors provide the foundation for personality traits, environmental influences, such as upbringing, culture, and life experiences, play a crucial role in shaping and modifying these traits over time.

One of the most influential theories in understanding personality is the Five Factor Model, also known as the Big Five. This model posits that personality can be distilled into five broad dimensions: openness to experience, conscientiousness, extraversion, agreeableness, and neuroticism. Each dimension represents a spectrum, with individuals falling at various points along the continuum. For example, someone high in openness may be imaginative and curious, while someone low in this trait may prefer routine and familiarity. The Big Five provides a comprehensive framework for understanding the diverse range of human personalities and offers insights into how these traits influence behavior and interpersonal relationships.

Personality is not static; it evolves over time. Life experiences, personal growth, and changing circumstances can lead to shifts in personality traits. This dynamic nature of personality underscores the importance of adaptability and resilience in navigating life's challenges. It also highlights the potential for personal transformation and growth. By understanding the factors that contribute to personality development, individuals can gain greater self-awareness and take proactive steps to cultivate desired traits and behaviors.

Culture and society play a significant role in shaping personality. Cultural norms, values, and expectations influence how individuals perceive themselves and others. They also dictate acceptable behaviors and social roles. For instance, collectivist cultures, which emphasize group harmony and interdependence, may foster traits such as agreeableness and cooperation. In contrast, individualistic cultures, which prioritize personal achievement and autonomy, may encourage traits like assertiveness and independence. Understanding the cultural context in which personality develops is essential for appreciating the diversity of human behavior and the ways in which individuals navigate their social environments.

Historical perspectives on personality development provide valuable insights into how our understanding of personality has evolved over time. Ancient philosophers, such as Hippocrates and Galen, proposed early theories of personality based on bodily humors. These ideas laid the groundwork for later psychological theories that sought to explain the complexities of human behavior. The emergence of psychoanalytic theory, spearheaded by Sigmund Freud, introduced the concept of the unconscious mind and its influence on personality. Freud's work paved the way for subsequent theories, such as behaviorism, humanism, and cognitive psychology, each offering unique perspectives on personality and its development.

The role of personality in shaping our lives cannot be overstated. It influences our choices, relationships, and overall well-being. Individuals with certain personality traits may be more predisposed to success in specific careers or social settings. For example, extraverts may thrive in roles that require social interaction and networking, while introverts may excel in solitary or analytical tasks. Understanding one's personality can provide valuable insights into personal strengths and areas for growth, enabling individuals to make informed decisions about their personal and professional lives.

Personality also plays a crucial role in mental health. Certain personality traits, such as high neuroticism or low conscientiousness, have been linked to an increased risk of mental health disorders, including anxiety and depression. Conversely, traits like resilience and emotional stability can serve as protective factors against stress and adversity. By recognizing the connection between personality and mental health, individuals can develop strategies to enhance their well-being and build resilience in the face of life's challenges.

The concept of personality is not limited to individual traits; it also encompasses the dynamic interactions between individuals and their environments. These interactions shape how personality is expressed and perceived by others. Social roles, relationships, and situational contexts can influence how personality traits manifest in different settings. For example, a person may exhibit high levels of agreeableness in personal relationships but adopt a more assertive demeanor in professional settings. Understanding these contextual influences is essential for appreciating the complexity of personality and its impact on behavior.

In the quest for personal transformation, understanding one's personality is a critical first step. Self-awareness allows individuals to identify their strengths and weaknesses, set meaningful goals, and develop strategies for personal growth. It also fosters empathy and understanding in interpersonal relationships, as individuals gain insight into the diverse personalities of those around them. By embracing the uniqueness of their personality, individuals can cultivate a sense of authenticity and purpose, leading to a more fulfilling and meaningful life.

The exploration of personality is a lifelong journey that offers endless opportunities for discovery and growth. It invites individuals to reflect on their experiences, challenge their assumptions, and embrace the complexity of human nature. By understanding the concept of personality, individuals can unlock their potential, navigate the intricacies of social interactions, and embark on a path of personal transformation.

The Importance of Standing Out

In a world teeming with billions of individuals, each striving to carve out their own niche, the importance of standing out cannot be overstated. The ability to distinguish oneself from the crowd is not merely a matter of personal pride; it is a crucial factor in achieving success, fulfillment, and recognition in various aspects of life. Whether in personal relationships, professional endeavors, or creative pursuits, standing out is the key to making a lasting impact and leaving a memorable impression.

The journey to standing out begins with self-awareness. Understanding one's unique strengths, talents, and passions is the foundation upon which individuality is built. It requires introspection and a willingness to embrace one's authentic self, free from the constraints of societal expectations or external pressures. By recognizing and valuing their distinct qualities, individuals can cultivate a sense of confidence and self-assurance that sets them apart from others.

Standing out is not about conforming to a predefined mold or adhering to conventional norms. It is about daring to be different and embracing one's uniqueness. This often involves taking risks and stepping outside of one's comfort zone. It requires the courage to challenge the status quo and pursue paths that may be unconventional or uncharted. By doing so, individuals can break free from the limitations of conformity and discover new opportunities for growth and self-expression.

In the professional realm, standing out is essential for career advancement and success. In a competitive job market, individuals who can differentiate themselves from their peers are more likely to capture the attention of employers and secure coveted positions. This differentiation can be achieved through a combination of skills, experiences, and personal attributes that align with the demands of the industry. Building a strong personal brand, showcasing unique talents, and demonstrating a commitment to continuous learning and development are effective strategies for standing out in the workplace.

Creativity and innovation are powerful tools for standing out. In a world where originality is highly valued, individuals who can think outside the box and offer fresh perspectives are often celebrated and sought after. Creativity is not limited to artistic endeavors; it can be applied to problem-solving, strategic thinking, and decision-making in various fields. By nurturing their creative instincts and embracing a mindset of curiosity and exploration, individuals can set themselves apart as visionary thinkers and trailblazers.

The importance of standing out extends beyond professional achievements; it also plays a vital role in personal relationships and social interactions. In a society that often prioritizes superficial connections, individuals who can forge genuine, meaningful relationships stand out as beacons of authenticity and empathy. By cultivating qualities such as active listening, empathy, and emotional intelligence, individuals can build strong, lasting connections with others and create a positive impact in their communities.

Standing out is not synonymous with seeking attention or validation from others. It is about being true to oneself and living in alignment with one's values and beliefs. It involves making choices that reflect one's authentic self, even if they go against the grain or defy conventional wisdom. By staying true to their principles and pursuing their passions with integrity, individuals can inspire others and leave a lasting legacy.

The journey to standing out is not without its challenges. It requires resilience and perseverance in the face of adversity and setbacks. Individuals who dare to be different may encounter resistance or criticism from those who are uncomfortable with change or threatened by innovation. However, by remaining steadfast in their convictions and maintaining a positive outlook, individuals can overcome obstacles and continue to shine brightly in their chosen paths.

In a rapidly changing world, the ability to adapt and evolve is crucial for standing out. Flexibility and openness to new experiences and ideas enable individuals to stay relevant and thrive in dynamic environments. By embracing change and viewing it as an opportunity for growth, individuals can continuously reinvent themselves and remain at the forefront of their fields.

Ultimately, the importance of standing out lies in the ability to make a meaningful contribution to the world. It is about using one's unique talents and perspectives to effect positive change and leave a lasting impact. Whether through innovation, leadership, or acts of kindness, individuals who stand out have the power to inspire others and create a ripple effect that extends far beyond their immediate sphere of influence.

Standing out is a lifelong journey of self-discovery and personal growth. It is an invitation to explore the depths of one's potential and embrace the richness of human diversity. By celebrating their individuality and daring to be different, individuals can unlock their full potential and lead lives of purpose and fulfillment.

Historical Perspectives on Personality Development

The exploration of personality development through history reveals a fascinating tapestry of ideas and theories that have evolved over centuries. From ancient philosophical musings to modern psychological frameworks, the understanding of personality has been shaped by diverse cultural, scientific, and intellectual influences. This historical journey not only highlights the complexity of human nature but also underscores the enduring quest to comprehend the essence of individuality.

In ancient times, the concept of personality was often intertwined with notions of temperament and character. The Greek physician Hippocrates, often regarded as the father of medicine, proposed one of the earliest theories of personality based on the balance of bodily humors. According to Hippocrates, the four humors—blood, phlegm, yellow bile, and black bile—determined an individual's temperament and behavior. This humoral theory laid the groundwork for subsequent explorations into the biological underpinnings of personality.

Building on Hippocrates' ideas, the Roman physician Galen expanded the theory of humors by associating each with specific personality traits. For instance, an excess of blood was thought to produce a sanguine temperament, characterized by optimism and sociability, while an abundance of black bile was linked to a melancholic disposition, marked by introspection and sensitivity. Although these early theories lacked empirical support, they provided a framework for understanding the diversity of human personalities and their potential impact on behavior.

The Middle Ages saw a shift in focus from biological explanations to spiritual and moral considerations. During this period, personality was often viewed through the lens of religious doctrine, with an emphasis on virtues and vices. Theologians and philosophers, such as St. Augustine and Thomas Aquinas, explored the moral dimensions of personality, emphasizing the role of free will and divine influence in shaping character. This perspective highlighted the interplay between individual agency and external forces in the development of personality.

The Renaissance marked a resurgence of interest in the study of human nature, driven by a renewed emphasis on observation and empirical inquiry. Thinkers like Leonardo da Vinci and Michel de Montaigne began to explore the complexities of personality through art, literature, and introspection. This period also saw the emergence of the concept of the "Renaissance man," an individual who embodied a diverse range of talents and interests, reflecting the multifaceted nature of personality.

The Enlightenment brought a more scientific approach to the study of personality, as philosophers and scientists sought to understand the human mind through reason and observation. The work of John Locke, who proposed the idea of the mind as a "tabula rasa" or blank slate, emphasized the role of experience and environment in shaping personality. This perspective laid the foundation for later theories that explored the influence of nurture on personality development.

The 19th century witnessed the rise of psychology as a distinct scientific discipline, with pioneers like Wilhelm Wundt and William James making significant contributions to the study of personality. Wundt's establishment of the first psychology laboratory in Leipzig marked a turning point in the empirical investigation of human behavior, while James' exploration of consciousness and individual differences laid the groundwork for future research on personality traits.

Sigmund Freud's psychoanalytic theory, which emerged in the late 19th and early 20th centuries, revolutionized the understanding of personality by introducing the concept of the unconscious mind. Freud's model of personality, comprising the id, ego, and superego, emphasized the dynamic interplay between instinctual drives, rational thought, and moral values. His work highlighted the influence of early childhood experiences and unconscious conflicts on personality development, paving the way for subsequent theories that explored the depths of the human psyche.

The mid-20th century saw the emergence of several influential theories of personality, each offering unique insights into the nature of individual differences. Carl Jung's analytical psychology introduced the concepts of archetypes and the collective unconscious, emphasizing the role of universal symbols and cultural influences in shaping personality. Meanwhile, Alfred Adler's individual psychology focused on the importance of social interest and the striving for superiority as key drivers of personality development.

The humanistic perspective, championed by theorists like Carl Rogers and Abraham Maslow, offered a more optimistic view of personality, emphasizing the potential for growth and self-actualization. Rogers' person-centered approach highlighted the importance of unconditional positive regard and empathy in fostering personal development, while Maslow's hierarchy of needs underscored the role of self-fulfillment in achieving one's full potential.

The latter half of the 20th century saw the rise of trait theories, which sought to identify and measure stable personality characteristics. The Five Factor Model, also known as the Big Five, emerged as a dominant framework for understanding personality, positing that individual differences could be captured by five broad dimensions: openness, conscientiousness, extraversion, agreeableness, and neuroticism. This model provided a comprehensive and empirically supported framework for studying personality across diverse populations and contexts.

As the field of psychology continues to evolve, contemporary research on personality development increasingly incorporates insights from neuroscience, genetics, and cross-cultural studies. Advances in brain imaging and genetic analysis have shed light on the biological underpinnings of personality traits, while cross-cultural research has highlighted the influence of cultural norms and values on personality expression.

The historical perspectives on personality development reveal a rich tapestry of ideas and theories that have shaped our understanding of human nature. From ancient humoral theories to modern trait models, each perspective has contributed to a more nuanced and comprehensive understanding of the factors that shape personality. This historical journey underscores the complexity of human individuality and the enduring quest to unravel the mysteries of the human mind.

The Role of Culture and Society

Culture and society are the intricate tapestries that weave together the fabric of human personality. They provide the context in which individuals develop, influencing their beliefs, behaviors, and identities. The role of culture and society in shaping personality is profound, as they dictate the norms, values, and expectations that guide human interactions and personal development. Understanding this dynamic interplay is essential for appreciating the diversity of human personalities and the ways in which individuals navigate their social environments.

Culture can be understood as the shared set of beliefs, customs, practices, and social behaviors of a particular group or society. It encompasses everything from language and religion to art and cuisine, forming the backdrop against which individuals live their lives. Culture provides a framework for understanding the world and one's place within it, offering a sense of identity and belonging. It influences how individuals perceive themselves and others, shaping their values, attitudes, and behaviors.

Society, on the other hand, refers to the organized community of individuals who share a common culture and interact with one another. It is the structure within which social relationships are formed and maintained, governed by rules, institutions, and hierarchies. Society provides the context for socialization, the process by which individuals learn and internalize the norms and values of their culture. Through socialization, individuals acquire the skills and knowledge necessary to function effectively within their social groups.

The influence of culture and society on personality begins at birth and continues throughout an individual's life. From the moment a child is born, they are immersed in a cultural environment that shapes their development. Family, as the primary agent of socialization, plays a crucial role in transmitting cultural values and norms to the child. Parents and caregivers impart beliefs, traditions, and customs, instilling a sense of cultural identity and belonging. Through interactions with family members, children learn the language, behaviors, and social roles expected of them within their culture.

As children grow, their socialization extends beyond the family to include other agents, such as schools, peers, and media. Educational institutions play a significant role in shaping personality by reinforcing cultural norms and values. Schools provide a structured environment where children learn to interact with others, develop social skills, and acquire knowledge about their culture and society. Peers also exert a powerful influence on personality development, as individuals seek acceptance and validation from their social groups. Peer interactions provide opportunities for individuals to explore different aspects of their personality and experiment with new behaviors.

Media, in its various forms, is a pervasive force in modern society that shapes cultural perceptions and influences personality. Television, films, music, and social media platforms expose individuals to a wide range of cultural messages and ideals. These media representations can reinforce or challenge cultural norms, shaping individuals' beliefs and attitudes. For example, media portrayals of gender roles, beauty standards, and success can impact individuals' self-perceptions and aspirations, influencing their personality development.

Cultural norms and values play a significant role in shaping personality by dictating acceptable behaviors and social roles. Different cultures prioritize different traits and behaviors, leading to variations in personality expression. For instance, collectivist cultures, which emphasize group harmony and interdependence, may foster traits such as agreeableness, cooperation, and conformity. In contrast, individualistic cultures, which prioritize personal achievement and autonomy, may encourage traits like assertiveness, independence, and self-reliance. Understanding these cultural differences is essential for appreciating the diversity of human personalities and the ways in which individuals navigate their social environments.

The role of culture and society in shaping personality is not limited to the transmission of norms and values; it also involves the negotiation of identity and self-concept. Individuals are active agents in their own development, constantly interpreting and responding to the cultural messages they encounter. This process of negotiation involves balancing personal desires and aspirations with societal expectations and constraints. It requires individuals to navigate the complexities of cultural identity, often leading to the development of a multifaceted and dynamic self-concept.

Cultural identity is a central aspect of personality, providing individuals with a sense of belonging and continuity. It encompasses the values, beliefs, and practices that individuals identify with and consider important to their sense of self. Cultural identity is not static; it evolves over time as individuals encounter new experiences and influences. This dynamic nature of cultural identity highlights the importance of adaptability and resilience in navigating the complexities of modern society.

The interplay between culture, society, and personality is further complicated by the phenomenon of globalization. In an increasingly interconnected world, individuals are exposed to a diverse array of cultural influences and perspectives. Globalization has led to the blending and fusion of cultures, creating opportunities for cross-cultural exchange and understanding. However, it has also raised challenges related to cultural identity and the preservation of cultural heritage. Individuals must navigate these complexities, balancing the desire for cultural integration with the need to maintain a sense of cultural distinctiveness.

The role of culture and society in shaping personality is a testament to the complexity and diversity of human nature. It underscores the importance of understanding the cultural context in which individuals develop and the ways in which cultural norms and values influence personality expression. By appreciating the intricate interplay between culture, society, and personality, individuals can gain greater insight into their own development and the diverse experiences of others. This understanding fosters empathy, tolerance, and respect for cultural diversity, promoting a more harmonious and inclusive society.

Setting the Stage for Personal Transformation

Personal transformation is a journey that begins with a single, often profound, realization: the desire for change. This desire can stem from various sources—a yearning for growth, a response to life's challenges, or an aspiration to achieve one's fullest potential. Setting the stage for personal transformation involves creating an environment conducive to change, both internally and externally. It requires a commitment to self-discovery, a willingness to embrace new experiences, and the courage to step into the unknown.

The first step in setting the stage for personal transformation is cultivating self-awareness. This involves taking a deep, honest look at oneself, acknowledging strengths and weaknesses, and understanding the motivations that drive behavior. Self-awareness is the foundation upon which transformation is built, as it provides clarity and insight into the areas of life that require change. It encourages individuals to reflect on their values, beliefs, and goals, aligning them with their true selves.

Journaling is a powerful tool for enhancing self-awareness. By regularly writing down thoughts, feelings, and experiences, individuals can gain a deeper understanding of their inner world. This practice encourages introspection and helps identify patterns and triggers that may be hindering personal growth. Journaling also serves as a record of progress, allowing individuals to track their transformation journey and celebrate milestones along the way.

Once self-awareness is established, the next step is setting clear, achievable goals. Goals provide direction and purpose, serving as a roadmap for personal transformation. They should be specific, measurable, attainable, relevant, and time-bound (SMART), ensuring that they are realistic and actionable. Setting goals involves envisioning the desired outcome and breaking it down into manageable steps. This process requires individuals to prioritize their aspirations and focus their energy on what truly matters.

Visualization is a technique that can enhance goal-setting by creating a vivid mental image of the desired outcome. By imagining themselves achieving their goals, individuals can increase motivation and reinforce their commitment to change. Visualization helps bridge the gap between the present and the future, making the journey toward transformation more tangible and attainable.

Creating a supportive environment is crucial for personal transformation. This involves surrounding oneself with positive influences, including supportive friends, mentors, and communities that encourage growth and development. A nurturing environment provides the encouragement and accountability needed to stay on track and overcome obstacles. It also offers opportunities for learning and collaboration, fostering a sense of belonging and connection.

Mindfulness and meditation are practices that can enhance personal transformation by promoting mental clarity and emotional balance. Mindfulness involves being present in the moment, observing thoughts and feelings without judgment. This practice cultivates a sense of calm and focus, reducing stress and increasing resilience. Meditation, on the other hand, involves intentional concentration and relaxation, allowing individuals to connect with their inner selves and gain insight into their thoughts and emotions. Both practices encourage self-reflection and self-compassion, essential components of personal transformation.

Embracing change and adaptability is another key aspect of setting the stage for personal transformation. Change is an inevitable part of life, and the ability to adapt to new circumstances is crucial for growth. This requires a mindset shift, viewing change as an opportunity rather than a threat. By embracing change, individuals can open themselves to new experiences and possibilities, expanding their horizons and enhancing their personal development.

Resilience is the ability to bounce back from setbacks and challenges, an essential trait for personal transformation. Building resilience involves developing coping strategies and a positive outlook, enabling individuals to navigate difficulties with grace and determination. It requires a willingness to learn from failures and view them as stepping stones to success. Resilience fosters perseverance and grit, empowering individuals to stay committed to their transformation journey despite obstacles.

Creative expression is a powerful catalyst for personal transformation. Engaging in creative activities, such as art, music, writing, or dance, allows individuals to explore their emotions and express their authentic selves. Creativity encourages experimentation and innovation, fostering a sense of freedom and self-discovery. It provides an outlet for processing emotions and gaining new perspectives, facilitating personal growth and transformation.

Leveraging technology can also play a significant role in personal transformation. Digital tools and resources, such as online courses, apps, and virtual communities, offer opportunities for learning and self-improvement. Technology provides access to a wealth of information and support, enabling individuals to acquire new skills and knowledge. It also facilitates connection and collaboration, allowing individuals to engage with like-minded individuals and share their transformation journey.

Ultimately, setting the stage for personal transformation is about creating a life that aligns with one's true self and aspirations. It involves a commitment to continuous growth and self-improvement, embracing change, and cultivating a mindset of possibility and potential. By taking intentional steps toward transformation, individuals can unlock their full potential and lead lives of purpose and fulfillment. The journey may be challenging, but the rewards are immeasurable—a deeper understanding of oneself, a greater sense of empowerment, and the realization of one's dreams.

Exploring Personality Theories

The exploration of personality theories offers a fascinating glimpse into the diverse ways in which scholars and psychologists have sought to understand the complexities of human behavior and individuality. These theories provide frameworks for examining the myriad factors that contribute to the development and expression of personality, offering insights into the underlying mechanisms that drive human actions, thoughts, and emotions. By delving into these theories, individuals can gain a deeper understanding of themselves and others, enhancing their ability to navigate the intricacies of interpersonal relationships and personal growth.

One of the most enduring and influential theories of personality is Sigmund Freud's psychoanalytic theory. Freud proposed that personality is shaped by the dynamic interplay of three components: the id, ego, and superego. The id represents the primal, instinctual drives that seek immediate gratification, while the superego embodies the internalized moral standards and ideals. The ego, acting as a mediator, balances the demands of the id and superego, navigating the complexities of reality. Freud's theory emphasizes the role of unconscious processes and early childhood experiences in shaping personality, highlighting the influence of unresolved conflicts and repressed desires on behavior.

Building on Freud's work, Carl Jung developed analytical psychology, which introduced the concepts of the collective unconscious and archetypes. Jung believed that the collective unconscious is a reservoir of shared memories and experiences inherited from our ancestors, influencing personality through universal symbols and motifs. Archetypes, such as the hero, the shadow, and the anima/animus, are innate, universal prototypes that shape individual behavior and experiences. Jung's theory emphasizes the importance of individuation, the process of integrating these archetypes into a cohesive self, as a key aspect of personality development.

Alfred Adler, another prominent figure in the field of psychology, proposed the theory of individual psychology, which focuses on the importance of social interest and the striving for superiority. Adler believed that individuals are motivated by a desire to overcome feelings of inferiority and achieve personal significance. This drive for superiority is expressed through unique life goals and personal values, shaping personality and behavior. Adler's theory highlights the role of social relationships and community involvement in personality development, emphasizing the interconnectedness of individuals and their environments.

The humanistic perspective, championed by theorists such as Carl Rogers and Abraham Maslow, offers a more optimistic view of personality, emphasizing the potential for growth and self-actualization. Rogers' person-centered approach posits that individuals possess an innate drive toward self-improvement and fulfillment. He emphasized the importance of unconditional positive regard, empathy, and authenticity in fostering personal growth and development. Maslow's hierarchy of needs, a cornerstone of humanistic psychology, outlines a progression of needs that individuals must satisfy to achieve self-actualization, the realization of one's fullest potential.

Trait theories, which focus on identifying and measuring stable personality characteristics, have become a dominant framework for understanding personality. The Five Factor Model, also known as the Big Five, posits that personality can be distilled into five broad dimensions: openness, conscientiousness, extraversion, agreeableness, and neuroticism. Each dimension represents a spectrum, with individuals falling at various points along the continuum. This model provides a comprehensive and empirically supported framework for studying personality across diverse populations and contexts, offering insights into how these traits influence behavior and interpersonal relationships.

Behaviorist theories, such as those proposed by B.F. Skinner and John Watson, emphasize the role of environmental influences and learning in shaping personality. According to behaviorism, personality is a result of learned behaviors and responses to external stimuli. Skinner's operant conditioning theory posits that behavior is shaped by reinforcement and punishment, with individuals learning to associate certain actions with positive or negative outcomes. This perspective highlights the importance of environmental factors and experiences in shaping personality, emphasizing the potential for change and adaptation through learning.

Cognitive theories of personality, such as those developed by Albert Bandura and George Kelly, focus on the role of cognitive processes in shaping personality. Bandura's social cognitive theory emphasizes the importance of observational learning, self-efficacy, and reciprocal determinism in personality development. According to Bandura, individuals learn by observing others and modeling their behavior, with self-efficacy beliefs influencing their ability to achieve goals and overcome challenges. Kelly's personal construct theory posits that individuals develop unique cognitive frameworks, or personal constructs, to interpret and predict events, shaping their perceptions and interactions with the world.

The exploration of personality theories reveals a rich tapestry of ideas and perspectives that have shaped our understanding of human nature. Each theory offers unique insights into the factors that influence personality development, highlighting the complexity and diversity of human behavior. By examining these theories, individuals can gain a deeper understanding of themselves and others, enhancing their ability to navigate the intricacies of interpersonal relationships and personal growth.

The integration of these diverse theories provides a more comprehensive understanding of personality, acknowledging the interplay of biological, psychological, and social factors in shaping individual differences. This holistic perspective emphasizes the importance of considering multiple influences and perspectives when examining personality, fostering a more nuanced and empathetic understanding of human behavior.

Ultimately, the exploration of personality theories is a journey of self-discovery and personal growth. By delving into these theories, individuals can gain valuable insights into their own personalities, enhancing their self-awareness and empowering them to make informed choices about their personal and professional lives. This journey invites individuals to reflect on their experiences, challenge their assumptions, and embrace the complexity of human nature, leading to a more fulfilling and meaningful life.

Nature vs. Nurture: The Debate

The nature versus nurture debate is one of the most enduring and complex discussions in the field of psychology, exploring the relative contributions of genetic inheritance and environmental factors to human development. This debate seeks to unravel the intricate interplay between biology and experience, examining how each shapes personality, behavior, and individual differences. Understanding this dynamic relationship is crucial for appreciating the diversity of human nature and the factors that influence personal growth and development.

Nature refers to the genetic and biological factors that contribute to an individual's development. These include inherited traits, genetic predispositions, and biological processes that influence physical and psychological characteristics. Proponents of the nature perspective argue that genetic makeup plays a significant role in determining personality traits, intelligence, and behavior. They emphasize the influence of heredity and biological factors, suggesting that many aspects of human development are predetermined by genetic inheritance.

Research in the field of behavioral genetics has provided valuable insights into the role of nature in shaping personality and behavior. Twin studies, which compare the similarities between identical and fraternal twins, have been instrumental in examining the heritability of various traits. These studies have shown that genetic factors account for a significant portion of the variance in traits such as intelligence, temperament, and personality. For example, identical twins, who share 100% of their genetic material, tend to exhibit more similar traits than fraternal twins, who share only 50% of their genes.

The influence of nature is also evident in the study of temperament, which refers to the innate aspects of an individual's personality, such as emotional reactivity and self-regulation. Research has shown that temperament is largely influenced by genetic factors, with certain traits, such as introversion and extraversion, being evident from early childhood. These findings suggest that biological predispositions play a crucial role in shaping personality and behavior, providing a foundation upon which environmental influences can build.

Nurture, on the other hand, refers to the environmental factors and experiences that shape an individual's development. These include family dynamics, cultural influences, education, and social interactions. Proponents of the nurture perspective argue that environmental factors play a significant role in shaping personality, behavior, and individual differences. They emphasize the importance of learning, experience, and socialization in influencing human development.

The role of nurture is evident in the process of socialization, through which individuals learn and internalize the norms, values, and behaviors of their culture. Family, as the primary agent of socialization, plays a crucial role in shaping an individual's personality and behavior. Parents and caregivers impart cultural values, beliefs, and practices, influencing the development of social skills, moral values, and self-concept. The impact of nurture is also evident in the influence of peers, education, and media, which provide additional opportunities for learning and socialization.

Environmental factors can also have a profound impact on cognitive development and intelligence. Research has shown that enriched environments, characterized by stimulating experiences and opportunities for learning, can enhance cognitive abilities and promote intellectual growth. Conversely, deprived environments, characterized by a lack of stimulation and resources, can hinder cognitive development and limit potential. These findings highlight the importance of environmental influences in shaping intellectual and cognitive outcomes.

The nature versus nurture debate is further complicated by the concept of gene-environment interaction, which suggests that genetic and environmental factors do not operate independently but interact in complex ways to influence development. This perspective emphasizes the dynamic interplay between biology and experience, suggesting that genetic predispositions can be modified or enhanced by environmental influences. For example, an individual with a genetic predisposition for high intelligence may achieve their full potential in an enriched environment that provides opportunities for learning and growth.

Epigenetics, the study of changes in gene expression caused by environmental factors, provides further evidence of the intricate relationship between nature and nurture. Epigenetic research has shown that environmental influences, such as diet, stress, and exposure to toxins, can alter gene expression and impact development. These findings suggest that environmental factors can have a lasting impact on genetic expression, highlighting the importance of considering both nature and nurture in understanding human development.

The nature versus nurture debate has significant implications for various fields, including psychology, education, and public policy. Understanding the relative contributions of genetic and environmental factors can inform approaches to education, mental health, and social interventions. For example, recognizing the role of environmental influences in cognitive development can inform educational practices that promote enriched learning environments and support diverse learning needs.

In the realm of mental health, the nature versus nurture debate underscores the importance of considering both biological and environmental factors in understanding and treating psychological disorders. Many mental health conditions, such as depression and anxiety, are influenced by a combination of genetic predispositions and environmental stressors. A comprehensive approach to mental health care that addresses both biological and environmental factors can enhance treatment outcomes and promote overall well-being.

Ultimately, the nature versus nurture debate highlights the complexity and diversity of human development, emphasizing the need for a holistic understanding of the factors that shape personality and behavior. By considering the interplay between genetic and environmental influences, individuals can gain a deeper appreciation of the unique contributions of nature and nurture to their own development and the development of others. This understanding fosters empathy, tolerance, and respect for individual differences, promoting a more inclusive and harmonious society.

Psychological Assessments and Their Impact

Psychological assessments are powerful tools that provide valuable insights into an individual's cognitive, emotional, and behavioral functioning. These assessments are designed to evaluate various aspects of mental health and personality, offering a comprehensive understanding of an individual's strengths, weaknesses, and potential areas for growth. By utilizing standardized tests and measures, psychological assessments can inform diagnosis, treatment planning, and personal development, ultimately impacting an individual's life in profound ways.

The process of psychological assessment typically begins with a referral, often initiated by a mental health professional, educator, or medical practitioner. The purpose of the assessment is to gather information that can aid in understanding an individual's psychological functioning and guide decision-making. This process involves a combination of interviews, observations, and standardized tests, each contributing to a holistic view of the individual's mental health and personality.

One of the most widely used types of psychological assessments is intelligence testing. These tests, such as the Wechsler Adult Intelligence Scale (WAIS) and the Stanford-Binet Intelligence Scales, measure cognitive abilities, including reasoning, problem-solving, and memory. Intelligence tests provide valuable information about an individual's intellectual strengths and weaknesses, informing educational and occupational decisions. For example, intelligence testing can identify giftedness or learning disabilities, guiding interventions and support to enhance academic and personal success.

Personality assessments are another crucial component of psychological evaluation. These assessments aim to measure enduring personality traits and characteristics, providing insights into an individual's behavior, emotions, and interpersonal relationships. The Minnesota Multiphasic Personality Inventory (MMPI) and the Five Factor Model (FFM) are examples of widely used personality assessments. These tools help identify personality patterns and potential psychological disorders, informing treatment planning and personal development.

Projective tests, such as the Rorschach Inkblot Test and the Thematic Apperception Test (TAT), are used to explore an individual's unconscious thoughts and feelings. These assessments involve presenting ambiguous stimuli and interpreting the individual's responses, revealing underlying emotions, conflicts, and motivations. Projective tests can provide valuable insights into an individual's inner world, offering a deeper understanding of their psychological functioning.

Neuropsychological assessments are specialized evaluations that focus on understanding the relationship between brain function and behavior. These assessments are often used to evaluate cognitive impairments resulting from brain injuries, neurological disorders, or developmental conditions. Neuropsychological tests assess various cognitive domains, including attention, memory, language, and executive functioning. The results of these assessments can inform diagnosis, treatment planning, and rehabilitation, enhancing an individual's quality of life.

The impact of psychological assessments extends beyond diagnosis and treatment planning. These evaluations can empower individuals by increasing self-awareness and promoting personal growth. By gaining a deeper understanding of their cognitive and emotional functioning, individuals can make informed decisions about their personal and professional lives. Psychological assessments can also enhance self-esteem and confidence by highlighting strengths and areas of competence, encouraging individuals to pursue their goals and aspirations.

In educational settings, psychological assessments play a vital role in identifying students' needs and supporting their academic success. Assessments can identify learning disabilities, attention deficits, and other challenges that may impact a student's performance. By understanding these challenges, educators can implement targeted interventions and accommodations, fostering a supportive learning environment that promotes student achievement. Psychological assessments can also identify giftedness, guiding enrichment opportunities and advanced placement to nurture students' talents and potential.

In the workplace, psychological assessments can inform hiring decisions, employee development, and organizational planning. Assessments can evaluate candidates' suitability for specific roles, identifying individuals with the skills and traits necessary for success. Employee assessments can also inform professional development, guiding training and coaching to enhance performance and career advancement. By understanding employees' strengths and areas for growth, organizations can create a supportive and productive work environment that fosters employee satisfaction and retention.

Despite their many benefits, psychological assessments are not without limitations and ethical considerations. The accuracy and validity of assessments depend on the quality of the tests and the expertise of the evaluator. It is essential for assessments to be conducted by qualified professionals who adhere to ethical guidelines and standards. Informed consent, confidentiality, and cultural sensitivity are critical components of ethical assessment practice, ensuring that individuals' rights and dignity are respected throughout the evaluation process.

Cultural considerations are particularly important in psychological assessment, as cultural factors can influence individuals' responses and interpretations of test items. Assessments must be culturally sensitive and appropriate, taking into account the individual's cultural background and experiences. This requires evaluators to be knowledgeable about cultural differences and to use culturally adapted tests and measures when necessary. By considering cultural factors, assessments can provide a more accurate and meaningful understanding of an individual's psychological functioning.

The impact of psychological assessments is far-reaching, influencing various aspects of individuals' lives and contributing to their overall well-being. By providing valuable insights into cognitive, emotional, and behavioral functioning, assessments can inform diagnosis, treatment, and personal development, empowering individuals to achieve their fullest potential. The process of assessment is a collaborative journey, involving the individual, the evaluator, and other stakeholders, each contributing to a comprehensive understanding of the individual's unique strengths and challenges.

In conclusion, psychological assessments are essential tools that offer a wealth of information about an individual's mental health and personality. By understanding the impact of these assessments, individuals can make informed decisions about their personal and professional lives, enhancing their well-being and achieving their goals. The journey of assessment is one of discovery and growth, providing individuals with the insights and tools they need to navigate the complexities of life with confidence and resilience.

The Neuroscience Behind Personality

The intricate tapestry of human personality is woven from the threads of both biology and experience, with neuroscience offering profound insights into the biological underpinnings of personality. By examining the brain's structure and function, researchers have begun to unravel the complex neural mechanisms that contribute to individual differences in personality traits and behaviors. This exploration into the neuroscience behind personality not only enhances our understanding of human nature but also provides valuable implications for personal development and mental health.

At the heart of the neuroscience of personality lies the brain's intricate network of neurons and synapses, which communicate through electrical and chemical signals. This vast network is responsible for processing information, regulating emotions, and guiding behavior. The brain's structure and function are influenced by both genetic and environmental factors, shaping the unique patterns of neural activity that underlie personality traits.

One of the key areas of the brain involved in personality is the prefrontal cortex, located at the front of the brain. This region is responsible for higher-order cognitive functions, such as decision-making, impulse control, and social behavior. The prefrontal cortex plays a crucial role in regulating emotions and behavior, influencing traits such as conscientiousness and self-control. Research has shown that variations in the structure and function of the prefrontal cortex are associated with individual differences in personality, highlighting its importance in shaping behavior and decision-making.

The limbic system, a group of interconnected structures deep within the brain, is another critical component of the neural basis of personality. This system is involved in processing emotions and regulating mood, playing a significant role in traits such as extraversion and neuroticism. The amygdala, a key structure within the limbic system, is particularly important for emotional processing and response to stress. Studies have shown that individuals with heightened amygdala activity tend to exhibit higher levels of anxiety and emotional reactivity, suggesting a link between amygdala function and neuroticism.

Neurotransmitters, the chemical messengers that transmit signals between neurons, also play a vital role in shaping personality. Dopamine, a neurotransmitter associated with reward and pleasure, is linked to traits such as novelty-seeking and extraversion. Individuals with higher levels of dopamine activity tend to be more outgoing and adventurous, seeking new experiences and social interactions. Serotonin, another neurotransmitter, is involved in mood regulation and is associated with traits such as agreeableness and emotional stability. Variations in serotonin levels can influence mood and behavior, contributing to individual differences in personality.

The concept of brain plasticity, or the brain's ability to change and adapt in response to experience, is a crucial aspect of the neuroscience of personality. Brain plasticity allows for the modification of neural pathways and the formation of new connections, enabling individuals to learn and adapt to new situations. This adaptability is essential for personal growth and development, as it allows individuals to modify their behavior and personality in response to changing circumstances. The brain's plasticity highlights the dynamic nature of personality, emphasizing the potential for change and growth throughout the lifespan.

Genetic factors also play a significant role in the neuroscience of personality, influencing the structure and function of the brain. Twin studies have shown that genetic factors account for a substantial portion of the variance in personality traits, suggesting a strong hereditary component. Specific genes have been identified that are associated with neurotransmitter function and brain structure, providing insights into the biological basis of personality. However, it is important to note that genetic factors do not operate in isolation but interact with environmental influences to shape personality.

Environmental factors, such as early life experiences and social interactions, can have a profound impact on the brain and personality development. Experiences during critical periods of development can influence the formation of neural connections and the maturation of brain structures, shaping personality traits and behaviors. For example, early exposure to stress or trauma can affect the development of the limbic system, influencing emotional regulation and stress response. Positive experiences, such as supportive relationships and enriching environments, can promote healthy brain development and enhance personality traits such as resilience and empathy.

The neuroscience of personality has significant implications for mental health and personal development. By understanding the neural mechanisms underlying personality traits, researchers can develop targeted interventions and treatments for psychological disorders. For example, therapies that focus on modifying neural pathways and enhancing brain plasticity can promote positive changes in behavior and personality. Additionally, understanding the biological basis of personality can inform strategies for personal growth and self-improvement, empowering individuals to harness their unique strengths and potential.

In the realm of mental health, the neuroscience of personality underscores the importance of considering both biological and environmental factors in understanding and treating psychological disorders. Many mental health conditions, such as depression and anxiety, are influenced by a combination of genetic predispositions and environmental stressors. A comprehensive approach to mental health care that addresses both biological and environmental factors can enhance treatment outcomes and promote overall well-being.

The exploration of the neuroscience behind personality is a journey of discovery and understanding, offering valuable insights into the complex interplay between biology and experience. By examining the neural mechanisms that contribute to individual differences in personality, researchers can gain a deeper appreciation of the diversity and complexity of human nature. This understanding fosters empathy, tolerance, and respect for individual differences, promoting a more inclusive and harmonious society.

Ultimately, the neuroscience of personality highlights the dynamic and adaptable nature of human behavior, emphasizing the potential for growth and change throughout the lifespan. By embracing the insights gained from neuroscience, individuals can enhance their self-awareness and personal development, leading to a more fulfilling and meaningful life. The journey of understanding the neuroscience of personality is one of exploration and growth, providing individuals with the tools and insights they need to navigate the complexities of life with confidence and resilience.

How Personality Shapes Our Lives

Personality is the invisible thread that weaves through the fabric of our lives, influencing our thoughts, behaviors, and interactions with the world around us. It is the unique constellation of traits and characteristics that define who we are, shaping our experiences and guiding our choices. Understanding how personality shapes our lives offers valuable insights into the ways in which we navigate the complexities of human existence, impacting everything from our relationships and career paths to our personal growth and well-being.

At the core of personality are the enduring traits that influence how we perceive and respond to the world. These traits, such as openness, conscientiousness, extraversion, agreeableness, and neuroticism, form the foundation of our personality and guide our interactions with others. For instance, individuals high in extraversion tend to be outgoing and sociable, thriving in social settings and seeking out new experiences. In contrast, those high in introversion may prefer solitude and introspection, finding fulfillment in quieter, more reflective activities. These traits influence our social interactions, shaping the way we form and maintain relationships with others.

Personality also plays a significant role in shaping our career choices and professional success. Individuals high in conscientiousness, characterized by traits such as organization, diligence, and reliability, often excel in structured and detail-oriented professions. Their ability to plan and execute tasks efficiently makes them valuable assets in roles that require precision and accountability. On the other hand, those high in openness, with their creativity and curiosity, may be drawn to careers in the arts or sciences, where innovation and exploration are valued. Understanding our personality traits can guide us in choosing career paths that align with our strengths and interests, enhancing job satisfaction and success.

The influence of personality extends to our approach to problem-solving and decision-making. Individuals high in agreeableness, known for their empathy and cooperation, may prioritize harmony and consensus in group settings, seeking solutions that benefit the collective. In contrast, those high in neuroticism, who may experience heightened emotional reactivity, might approach decision-making with caution, considering potential risks and uncertainties. These differences in problem-solving styles can impact our ability to navigate challenges and adapt to change, influencing our resilience and coping strategies.

Personality also shapes our emotional experiences and well-being. Traits such as neuroticism and emotional stability play a crucial role in determining how we perceive and manage stress and adversity. Individuals high in neuroticism may be more prone to experiencing negative emotions, such as anxiety and depression, and may require additional support to develop effective coping mechanisms. Conversely, those high in emotional stability may exhibit greater resilience, maintaining a positive outlook even in the face of challenges. Understanding the impact of personality on emotional well-being can inform strategies for managing stress and enhancing mental health.

In the realm of personal growth and self-improvement, personality serves as both a guide and a catalyst for change. By gaining insight into our personality traits, we can identify areas for growth and development, setting goals that align with our values and aspirations. For example, individuals seeking to enhance their social skills may focus on developing traits such as extraversion and agreeableness, engaging in activities that promote social interaction and empathy. Similarly, those aiming to improve their organizational skills may work on cultivating conscientiousness, implementing strategies to enhance time management and productivity.

Personality also influences our values and beliefs, shaping the way we perceive and interpret the world. Traits such as openness and agreeableness can impact our attitudes toward diversity and inclusion, influencing our willingness to embrace new ideas and perspectives. Individuals high in openness may be more receptive to change and innovation, valuing creativity and exploration. In contrast, those high in agreeableness may prioritize harmony and cooperation, valuing relationships and community. Understanding the role of personality in shaping our values can enhance our ability to engage with others and contribute to a more inclusive and harmonious society.

The impact of personality on our lives is further illustrated through the lens of storytelling, where characters' traits and motivations drive the narrative and shape their journeys. Consider the classic tale of "Pride and Prejudice," where the protagonist, Elizabeth Bennet, navigates the complexities of love and social expectations. Her wit and independence, hallmarks of her personality, guide her interactions and decisions, ultimately leading to personal growth and fulfillment. Through stories like these, we see how personality influences the choices we make and the paths we take, shaping our destinies and defining our legacies.

In relationships, personality plays a pivotal role in determining compatibility and dynamics. Traits such as agreeableness and emotional stability can influence the quality and longevity of relationships, impacting communication, conflict resolution, and intimacy. Individuals high in agreeableness may prioritize empathy and understanding, fostering supportive and nurturing relationships. Conversely, those high in neuroticism may experience heightened emotional reactivity, requiring additional effort to manage conflicts and maintain harmony. Understanding the role of personality in relationships can inform strategies for building and sustaining healthy connections, enhancing interpersonal satisfaction and fulfillment.

The influence of personality on our lives is not static but dynamic, evolving over time as we grow and adapt to new experiences. Life events, such as career changes, relationships, and personal challenges, can shape and refine our personality traits, influencing our development and growth. By embracing the fluid nature of personality, we can cultivate a mindset of continuous learning and self-improvement, adapting to the ever-changing landscape of life with resilience and grace.

Ultimately, the exploration of how personality shapes our lives offers valuable insights into the complexities of human nature and the factors that influence our experiences and choices. By understanding the role of personality in shaping our thoughts, behaviors, and interactions, we can enhance our self-awareness and personal development, leading to a more fulfilling and meaningful life. The journey of understanding personality is one of discovery and growth, providing us with the tools and insights we need to navigate the complexities of life with confidence and resilience.

Chapter 3: Innovative Approaches to Personal Growth

Embracing Change and Adaptability

Change is an inevitable part of life, a constant force that shapes our experiences and challenges our perceptions. Embracing change and cultivating adaptability are essential skills for navigating the complexities of the modern world. These abilities empower individuals to respond effectively to new situations, overcome obstacles, and seize opportunities for growth and development. By understanding the dynamics of change and fostering a mindset of adaptability, we can enhance our resilience and thrive in an ever-evolving landscape.

The nature of change is multifaceted, encompassing both external and internal transformations. External changes may include shifts in the workplace, technological advancements, or societal trends, while internal changes involve personal growth, evolving beliefs, and emotional development. Regardless of the source, change often requires us to step outside our comfort zones and confront the unknown. This can be daunting, as uncertainty and unpredictability can evoke feelings of anxiety and resistance. However, by embracing change as an opportunity for growth, we can transform these challenges into catalysts for personal and professional development.

Adaptability is the ability to adjust to new conditions and respond effectively to change. It involves a combination of cognitive flexibility, emotional resilience, and behavioral agility.

Cognitive flexibility allows us to shift our thinking and consider alternative perspectives, enabling us to approach problems with creativity and innovation. Emotional resilience equips us to manage stress and maintain a positive outlook, even in the face of adversity. Behavioral agility empowers us to modify our actions and strategies, ensuring that we remain effective and responsive in dynamic environments.

One of the key components of adaptability is the willingness to learn and grow. This involves cultivating a growth mindset, which is the belief that abilities and intelligence can be developed through effort and perseverance. Individuals with a growth mindset view challenges as opportunities for learning and are more likely to embrace change with enthusiasm and curiosity. By adopting a growth mindset, we can enhance our adaptability and increase our capacity for personal and professional growth.

The process of embracing change and developing adaptability begins with self-awareness. By reflecting on our strengths, weaknesses, and areas for growth, we can identify the skills and resources needed to navigate change effectively. Self-awareness also involves recognizing our emotional responses to change and understanding how these emotions influence our behavior. By acknowledging and addressing our fears and anxieties, we can develop strategies to manage stress and build resilience.

Effective communication is another crucial aspect of adaptability. In times of change, clear and open communication can facilitate collaboration and foster a sense of shared purpose. By actively listening to others and expressing our thoughts and feelings, we can build trust and strengthen relationships. This collaborative approach can enhance our ability to adapt to new situations and work effectively with others to achieve common goals.

Flexibility in problem-solving is also essential for adaptability. This involves approaching challenges with an open mind and considering multiple solutions. By exploring different perspectives and experimenting with new approaches, we can develop innovative solutions and overcome obstacles. Flexibility in problem-solving also requires the ability to pivot and adjust strategies as needed, ensuring that we remain responsive and effective in changing circumstances.

The ability to embrace change and cultivate adaptability is not only beneficial for personal growth but also essential for professional success. In the workplace, adaptability is a highly valued skill, as it enables individuals to respond effectively to shifting priorities, evolving technologies, and changing market conditions. By demonstrating adaptability, individuals can enhance their career prospects and contribute to the success of their organizations.

To foster adaptability in the workplace, it is important to create an environment that encourages learning and innovation. This involves providing opportunities for professional development, promoting a culture of continuous improvement, and supporting employees in their efforts to adapt to change. By fostering a supportive and inclusive work environment, organizations can enhance their adaptability and resilience, ensuring long-term success in a rapidly changing world.

In addition to professional settings, adaptability is also crucial for personal relationships and social interactions. By being open to change and willing to adjust our behavior, we can build stronger and more meaningful connections with others. This involves being receptive to feedback, understanding different perspectives, and being willing to compromise and collaborate. By cultivating adaptability in our relationships, we can enhance our interpersonal skills and foster a sense of empathy and understanding.

The journey of embracing change and developing adaptability is a lifelong process, requiring ongoing reflection and growth. By remaining open to new experiences and willing to learn from both successes and failures, we can continue to enhance our adaptability and resilience. This journey is not without its challenges, but by approaching change with a positive and proactive mindset, we can transform obstacles into opportunities for growth and development.

Ultimately, embracing change and cultivating adaptability are essential skills for navigating the complexities of life. By understanding the dynamics of change and fostering a mindset of adaptability, we can enhance our resilience and thrive in an ever-evolving landscape. The journey of embracing change is one of discovery and growth, providing us with the tools and insights we need to navigate the complexities of life with confidence and resilience.

The Power of Mindfulness and Meditation

Mindfulness and meditation have emerged as powerful practices that offer profound benefits for mental, emotional, and physical well-being. Rooted in ancient traditions, these practices have gained widespread popularity in modern society as effective tools for managing stress, enhancing focus, and promoting overall health. By cultivating a state of present-moment awareness and fostering a deeper connection with oneself, mindfulness and meditation empower individuals to navigate the complexities of life with clarity and resilience.

At its core, mindfulness is the practice of paying attention to the present moment with an open and non-judgmental attitude. It involves observing thoughts, emotions, and sensations as they arise, without becoming attached or reactive. This heightened awareness allows individuals to break free from habitual patterns of thinking and behavior, creating space for intentional and conscious responses. By cultivating mindfulness, individuals can develop greater self-awareness and emotional regulation, enhancing their ability to cope with stress and adversity.

Meditation, a complementary practice to mindfulness, involves focused attention and concentration techniques to achieve a state of mental clarity and relaxation. There are various forms of meditation, each with its unique approach and benefits. Mindfulness meditation, for example, involves observing the breath or bodily sensations, anchoring the mind in the present moment. Loving-kindness meditation, on the other hand, focuses on cultivating compassion and empathy towards oneself and others. Regardless of the specific technique, meditation serves as a powerful tool for calming the mind and fostering a sense of inner peace.

The benefits of mindfulness and meditation extend beyond mental and emotional well-being, impacting physical health as well. Research has shown that regular practice can reduce symptoms of anxiety and depression, lower blood pressure, and improve immune function. By promoting relaxation and reducing stress, mindfulness and meditation can enhance overall health and vitality, contributing to a greater sense of well-being.

One of the key mechanisms through which mindfulness and meditation exert their effects is by modulating the body's stress response. In times of stress, the body activates the "fight or flight" response, releasing stress hormones such as cortisol and adrenaline. While this response is adaptive in short-term situations, chronic activation can lead to negative health outcomes, including increased risk of cardiovascular disease and weakened immune function. Mindfulness and meditation help counteract this response by activating the body's relaxation response, reducing stress hormone levels, and promoting a state of calm and balance.

In addition to their physiological benefits, mindfulness and meditation also enhance cognitive functioning and mental clarity. By training the mind to focus and sustain attention, these practices improve concentration and memory, enhancing productivity and performance. Mindfulness and meditation also promote cognitive flexibility, allowing individuals to approach problems with creativity and innovation. This enhanced mental agility can lead to more effective decision-making and problem-solving, contributing to personal and professional success.

The practice of mindfulness and meditation is accessible to individuals of all ages and backgrounds, requiring no special equipment or expertise. To begin, individuals can set aside a few minutes each day to engage in mindful breathing or meditation exercises. Finding a quiet and comfortable space, free from distractions, can enhance the effectiveness of the practice. As individuals become more familiar with the techniques, they can gradually increase the duration and frequency of their practice, integrating mindfulness and meditation into their daily routines.

For beginners, guided meditation sessions can provide valuable support and structure, offering step-by-step instructions and encouragement. Many resources, including apps and online platforms, offer guided meditations tailored to various needs and preferences. These resources can serve as helpful tools for establishing a consistent practice and exploring different meditation techniques.

Incorporating mindfulness into daily activities is another effective way to cultivate present-moment awareness. Simple practices, such as mindful eating or walking, involve bringing attention to the sensory experiences of the moment, fostering a deeper connection with the present. By integrating mindfulness into everyday tasks, individuals can enhance their awareness and appreciation of the world around them, enriching their overall experience of life.

The transformative power of mindfulness and meditation is further illustrated through personal stories and testimonials. Many individuals have reported profound changes in their lives as a result of regular practice, experiencing greater emotional balance, improved relationships, and a heightened sense of purpose and fulfillment. These stories serve as a testament to the potential of mindfulness and meditation to foster personal growth and transformation.

In the context of mental health, mindfulness and meditation offer valuable tools for managing symptoms and enhancing well-being. For individuals experiencing anxiety or depression, these practices can provide a sense of grounding and stability, reducing rumination and promoting positive emotions.

Mindfulness-based interventions, such as Mindfulness-Based Stress Reduction (MBSR) and Mindfulness-Based Cognitive Therapy (MBCT), have been shown to be effective in reducing symptoms and preventing relapse, offering a complementary approach to traditional therapies.

The power of mindfulness and meditation lies in their ability to cultivate a deeper connection with oneself and the present moment. By fostering awareness and acceptance, these practices empower individuals to navigate the complexities of life with clarity and resilience. The journey of mindfulness and meditation is one of self-discovery and growth, offering valuable insights and tools for enhancing well-being and achieving a more fulfilling and meaningful life.

Ultimately, the practice of mindfulness and meditation is a personal journey, unique to each individual. By embracing these practices with an open and curious mind, individuals can unlock their potential for growth and transformation, leading to a more balanced and harmonious life. The power of mindfulness and meditation is within reach for all who seek it, offering a path to greater awareness, peace, and fulfillment.

Leveraging Technology for Self-Improvement

In the digital age, technology has become an integral part of our daily lives, offering unprecedented opportunities for self-improvement and personal growth. From mobile apps and online courses to wearable devices and virtual communities, technology provides a wealth of resources and tools that can enhance our abilities, expand our knowledge, and support our well-being. By leveraging technology effectively, individuals can embark on a journey of self-discovery and development, unlocking their potential and achieving their goals.

One of the most accessible and versatile tools for self-improvement is the smartphone, a device that has revolutionized the way we access information and connect with others. With a myriad of apps designed to support personal growth, smartphones offer a convenient and portable platform for learning and development. Educational apps, for example, provide access to a vast array of subjects, from language learning and coding to mindfulness and fitness. These apps often incorporate interactive features, such as quizzes and games, to engage users and reinforce learning. By integrating educational apps into daily routines, individuals can acquire new skills and knowledge at their own pace, transforming idle moments into valuable learning opportunities.

In addition to educational apps, productivity tools can enhance time management and organization, helping individuals achieve their goals more efficiently. Calendar and task management apps, for instance, allow users to schedule activities, set reminders, and track progress, ensuring that important tasks are prioritized and completed on time. By utilizing these tools, individuals can optimize their workflows and reduce stress, creating a more balanced and productive lifestyle.

Wearable technology, such as fitness trackers and smartwatches, offers another avenue for self-improvement by promoting physical health and well-being. These devices monitor various health metrics, such as heart rate, sleep patterns, and physical activity, providing users with real-time feedback and insights. By tracking progress and setting personalized goals, individuals can make informed decisions about their health and fitness, fostering a sense of accountability and motivation. Wearable technology also encourages mindfulness and self-awareness, as users become more attuned to their bodies and habits.

Online courses and virtual learning platforms have democratized education, making high-quality learning experiences accessible to individuals worldwide. Platforms such as Coursera, Udemy, and Khan Academy offer a diverse range of courses, taught by experts in their respective fields. These courses often include video lectures, interactive assignments, and peer discussions, providing a comprehensive and engaging learning experience. By enrolling in online courses, individuals can pursue their interests and career aspirations, gaining valuable skills and credentials that enhance their personal and professional development.

Virtual communities and social networks also play a significant role in self-improvement by fostering connection and collaboration. Online forums, discussion groups, and social media platforms provide spaces for individuals to share experiences, seek advice, and offer support. These virtual communities can be particularly valuable for individuals pursuing specific goals, such as weight loss, entrepreneurship, or creative endeavors, as they offer a sense of camaraderie and accountability. By engaging with like-minded individuals, users can gain new perspectives, overcome challenges, and celebrate achievements, enhancing their motivation and resilience.

While technology offers numerous benefits for self-improvement, it is important to approach it with intention and mindfulness. The abundance of digital tools and information can be overwhelming, leading to distractions and information overload. To leverage technology effectively, individuals should set clear goals and priorities, selecting tools and resources that align with their objectives. By establishing boundaries and practicing digital mindfulness, users can maintain focus and balance, ensuring that technology serves as a support rather than a hindrance.

Privacy and security are also important considerations when using technology for self-improvement. As individuals share personal information and data with apps and online platforms, it is essential to be aware of privacy settings and data protection measures. By taking proactive steps to safeguard personal information, users can protect their privacy and maintain control over their digital identities.

The integration of technology into self-improvement practices is not without its challenges, but with thoughtful and intentional use, it can be a powerful catalyst for growth and transformation. By embracing the opportunities that technology offers, individuals can enhance their skills, expand their horizons, and achieve their aspirations. The journey of leveraging technology for self-improvement is one of exploration and empowerment, providing individuals with the tools and insights they need to navigate the complexities of life with confidence and resilience.

In the realm of mental health, technology offers innovative solutions for support and intervention. Mental health apps, for example, provide resources for managing stress, anxiety, and depression, offering guided meditations, mood tracking, and cognitive behavioral therapy exercises. These apps can serve as valuable complements to traditional therapy, providing users with accessible and convenient tools for self-care and emotional regulation. By incorporating mental health technology into their routines, individuals can enhance their well-being and build resilience, fostering a greater sense of balance and fulfillment.

The potential of technology for self-improvement extends to creative and artistic pursuits as well. Digital tools and platforms, such as graphic design software, music production apps, and online writing communities, offer opportunities for creative expression and collaboration. By exploring these tools, individuals can develop their artistic skills and share their creations with a global audience, gaining feedback and inspiration from others. Technology also enables individuals to connect with mentors and experts in their fields, providing valuable guidance and support for their creative journeys.

Ultimately, the power of technology for self-improvement lies in its ability to connect, educate, and empower individuals. By harnessing the potential of digital tools and resources, individuals can embark on a journey of self-discovery and growth, unlocking their potential and achieving their goals. The journey of leveraging technology for self-improvement is one of exploration and empowerment, providing individuals with the tools and insights they need to navigate the complexities of life with confidence and resilience.

Creative Expression as a Tool for Growth

Creative expression is a powerful conduit for personal growth, offering individuals a means to explore their inner worlds, communicate emotions, and foster self-discovery. Whether through art, music, writing, or dance, creative expression transcends the boundaries of language and culture, providing a universal platform for self-exploration and transformation. By engaging in creative activities, individuals can tap into their innate potential, cultivate resilience, and enhance their overall well-being.

At the heart of creative expression lies the ability to communicate complex emotions and ideas in a tangible form. This process of externalizing internal experiences allows individuals to gain insight into their thoughts and feelings, fostering a deeper understanding of themselves and their place in the world. For instance, a painter may use color and form to convey emotions that are difficult to articulate verbally, while a writer may craft narratives that explore personal experiences and challenges. Through these creative endeavors, individuals can process emotions, gain clarity, and find meaning in their experiences.

Creative expression also serves as a powerful tool for stress relief and emotional regulation. Engaging in creative activities can provide a sense of escape and relaxation, allowing individuals to disconnect from the pressures of daily life and immerse themselves in the present moment. This state of flow, characterized by complete absorption and focus, can lead to a reduction in stress and anxiety, promoting a sense of calm and well-being. Moreover, creative expression can serve as a healthy outlet for processing difficult emotions, enabling individuals to release pent-up feelings and gain perspective on their challenges.

The benefits of creative expression extend beyond emotional well-being, impacting cognitive functioning and problem-solving abilities. Creative activities stimulate the brain, enhancing neural connections and promoting cognitive flexibility. This mental agility allows individuals to approach problems with an open mind, exploring multiple solutions and thinking outside the box. By fostering creativity, individuals can develop innovative approaches to challenges, enhancing their ability to adapt and thrive in dynamic environments.

In addition to its cognitive benefits, creative expression fosters personal growth by encouraging exploration and experimentation. The creative process often involves taking risks, embracing uncertainty, and pushing the boundaries of one's comfort zone. This willingness to explore the unknown can lead to new insights and discoveries, fostering a sense of curiosity and wonder. By embracing the creative process, individuals can cultivate a growth mindset, viewing challenges as opportunities for learning and development.

Creative expression also plays a significant role in building self-confidence and self-esteem. As individuals engage in creative activities and witness their progress, they gain a sense of accomplishment and pride in their abilities. This positive reinforcement can boost self-esteem and encourage individuals to pursue their passions and interests with confidence. Moreover, sharing creative work with others can foster a sense of connection and validation, enhancing interpersonal relationships and social support.

The transformative power of creative expression is further illustrated through personal stories and testimonials. Many individuals have reported profound changes in their lives as a result of engaging in creative activities, experiencing greater self-awareness, emotional balance, and fulfillment. These stories serve as a testament to the potential of creative expression to foster personal growth and transformation.

In the context of mental health, creative expression offers valuable tools for healing and recovery. Art therapy, for example, utilizes creative expression as a therapeutic modality, helping individuals process trauma, manage symptoms, and enhance well-being. Through guided creative activities, individuals can explore their emotions and experiences in a safe and supportive environment, gaining insight and empowerment. By incorporating creative expression into mental health practices, individuals can enhance their resilience and foster a greater sense of balance and fulfillment.

The journey of creative expression is a personal and unique experience, shaped by individual interests, preferences, and goals. To begin, individuals can explore various creative activities, such as painting, writing, music, or dance, to discover what resonates with them. Setting aside dedicated time for creative pursuits can help establish a consistent practice, allowing individuals to immerse themselves in the process and reap the benefits of creative expression.

For beginners, workshops and classes can provide valuable guidance and support, offering structured opportunities to learn new skills and techniques. These settings also foster a sense of community and collaboration, allowing individuals to connect with others who share similar interests and passions. By participating in creative communities, individuals can gain inspiration, feedback, and encouragement, enhancing their creative journeys.

Ultimately, creative expression is a powerful tool for personal growth, offering individuals a means to explore their inner worlds, communicate emotions, and foster self-discovery. By engaging in creative activities, individuals can tap into their innate potential, cultivate resilience, and enhance their overall well-being. The journey of creative expression is one of exploration and empowerment, providing individuals with the tools and insights they need to navigate the complexities of life with confidence and resilience.

Building Resilience and Emotional Intelligence

Resilience and emotional intelligence are two intertwined qualities that play a crucial role in navigating life's challenges and maintaining mental well-being. In an ever-changing world, the ability to bounce back from adversity and understand one's own emotions, as well as those of others, is invaluable. These skills not only enhance personal growth but also improve relationships and professional success. By cultivating resilience and emotional intelligence, individuals can develop a robust foundation for a fulfilling and balanced life.

Resilience is the capacity to recover quickly from difficulties and adapt to change. It is not an innate trait but rather a skill that can be developed and strengthened over time. Resilient individuals possess a positive outlook, viewing setbacks as opportunities for growth rather than insurmountable obstacles. This mindset enables them to persevere in the face of adversity and emerge stronger from their experiences. Building resilience involves cultivating a range of skills, including problem-solving, adaptability, and self-regulation.

One of the key components of resilience is the ability to manage stress effectively. Stress is an inevitable part of life, but how we respond to it can significantly impact our well-being. Resilient individuals employ healthy coping strategies, such as exercise, mindfulness, and social support, to manage stress and maintain balance. By developing these coping mechanisms, individuals can enhance their resilience and reduce the negative impact of stress on their lives.

Another important aspect of resilience is the ability to maintain a sense of purpose and meaning. Resilient individuals often have a clear sense of their values and goals, which provides them with direction and motivation during challenging times. By aligning their actions with their values, individuals can cultivate a sense of fulfillment and satisfaction, even in the face of adversity. This sense of purpose serves as a guiding light, helping individuals navigate the complexities of life with confidence and determination.

Emotional intelligence, on the other hand, is the ability to recognize, understand, and manage one's own emotions, as well as the emotions of others. It involves a range of skills, including self-awareness, empathy, and effective communication. Emotionally intelligent individuals are adept at navigating social interactions, building strong relationships, and resolving conflicts. By enhancing emotional intelligence, individuals can improve their interpersonal skills and foster a greater sense of connection and understanding.

Self-awareness is a fundamental component of emotional intelligence, involving the ability to recognize and understand one's own emotions and their impact on behavior. By cultivating self-awareness, individuals can gain insight into their emotional triggers and patterns, enabling them to respond to situations with greater intention and control. This heightened awareness also allows individuals to identify areas for growth and development, fostering personal and professional growth.

Empathy, another key aspect of emotional intelligence, involves the ability to understand and share the feelings of others. Empathetic individuals are skilled at reading social cues and responding to the emotions of others with compassion and understanding. By cultivating empathy, individuals can build stronger and more meaningful relationships, enhancing their social support networks and overall well-being.

Effective communication is also essential for emotional intelligence, involving the ability to express emotions and thoughts clearly and constructively. Emotionally intelligent individuals are skilled at active listening, ensuring that they understand the perspectives and needs of others. By fostering open and honest communication, individuals can resolve conflicts and build trust, enhancing their relationships and social interactions.

The development of resilience and emotional intelligence is a lifelong journey, requiring ongoing reflection and practice. To begin, individuals can engage in self-reflection and mindfulness practices to enhance self-awareness and emotional regulation. Journaling, meditation, and mindfulness exercises can provide valuable insights into one's emotions and thought patterns, fostering greater self-understanding and control.

Building a strong support network is also crucial for developing resilience and emotional intelligence. By cultivating meaningful relationships with family, friends, and colleagues, individuals can gain valuable support and encouragement during challenging times. These connections provide a sense of belonging and security, enhancing resilience and emotional well-being.

In addition to personal practices, professional development opportunities can also enhance resilience and emotional intelligence. Workshops, courses, and coaching sessions can provide valuable tools and strategies for building these skills, offering structured opportunities for growth and learning. By investing in personal and professional development, individuals can enhance their resilience and emotional intelligence, leading to greater success and fulfillment in all areas of life.

The benefits of resilience and emotional intelligence extend beyond personal well-being, impacting professional success and leadership. In the workplace, resilient and emotionally intelligent individuals are better equipped to handle stress, adapt to change, and collaborate effectively with others. These skills are highly valued by employers, as they contribute to a positive and productive work environment. By cultivating resilience and emotional intelligence, individuals can enhance their career prospects and contribute to the success of their organizations.

The journey of building resilience and emotional intelligence is one of self-discovery and growth, offering valuable insights and tools for navigating the complexities of life. By embracing these qualities, individuals can enhance their well-being, improve their relationships, and achieve their goals. The development of resilience and emotional intelligence is a lifelong process, providing individuals with the foundation they need to thrive in an ever-changing world.

Chapter 4: Tailoring Personality Development for Men

Understanding Male Archetypes

Male archetypes have long been a subject of fascination and study, offering insights into the diverse expressions of masculinity and the roles men play in society. These archetypes, rooted in mythology, literature, and psychology, serve as symbolic representations of universal patterns and behaviors. By understanding male archetypes, individuals can gain a deeper awareness of their own identities and the cultural narratives that shape their experiences. This exploration can foster personal growth, self-acceptance, and a more nuanced understanding of masculinity.

The concept of archetypes was popularized by Swiss psychologist Carl Jung, who identified them as recurring symbols and motifs that reside in the collective unconscious. According to Jung, archetypes are innate, universal prototypes for ideas and may be used to interpret observations. In the context of masculinity, male archetypes represent different facets of the male experience, each embodying distinct qualities, strengths, and challenges. These archetypes can be seen as guiding forces, influencing how men perceive themselves and navigate the world.

One of the most well-known male archetypes is the Warrior, characterized by strength, courage, and a sense of duty. The Warrior embodies the protector and defender, willing to fight for what is right and just. This archetype is often associated with physical prowess and bravery, but it also encompasses mental fortitude and resilience. The Warrior's journey involves mastering discipline and harnessing aggression in constructive ways. While the Warrior can be a powerful force for good, it also carries the risk of becoming overly aggressive or domineering if not balanced with empathy and compassion.

The King archetype represents leadership, authority, and responsibility. As a ruler, the King embodies wisdom, fairness, and the ability to create order and stability. This archetype is associated with the qualities of a benevolent leader who serves the greater good and inspires others to reach their potential. The King's journey involves cultivating integrity, vision, and the ability to make difficult decisions. However, the shadow side of the King can manifest as tyranny or arrogance if power is abused or unchecked.

The Magician archetype is characterized by intellect, creativity, and transformation. The Magician is a seeker of knowledge and a master of change, using insight and innovation to solve problems and create new possibilities. This archetype is associated with the qualities of curiosity, adaptability, and the ability to see beyond the ordinary. The Magician's journey involves embracing the unknown and using wisdom to bring about positive change. The shadow side of the Magician can emerge as manipulation or deceit if knowledge is used for selfish or harmful purposes.

The Lover archetype embodies passion, connection, and emotional depth. The Lover is attuned to beauty, pleasure, and the richness of human experience, seeking meaningful relationships and experiences. This archetype is associated with qualities of empathy, sensitivity, and the ability to form deep bonds with others. The Lover's journey involves embracing vulnerability and cultivating intimacy and compassion. However, the shadow side of the Lover can manifest as obsession or dependency if emotions are not balanced with reason and self-awareness.

The Explorer archetype represents adventure, curiosity, and the pursuit of new experiences. The Explorer is driven by a desire to discover the unknown and expand horizons, both physically and intellectually. This archetype is associated with qualities of independence, courage, and a willingness to take risks. The Explorer's journey involves embracing change and seeking personal growth through exploration. The shadow side of the Explorer can emerge as restlessness or avoidance if the pursuit of novelty leads to a lack of commitment or responsibility.

Understanding male archetypes can provide valuable insights into the complexities of masculinity and the diverse ways it is expressed. By recognizing these archetypes within themselves, individuals can gain a deeper understanding of their strengths, challenges, and potential for growth. This awareness can foster self-acceptance and authenticity, allowing individuals to embrace their unique identities and navigate the world with confidence.

The exploration of male archetypes also offers an opportunity to challenge and redefine traditional notions of masculinity. In contemporary society, rigid gender roles and stereotypes can limit self-expression and perpetuate harmful behaviors. By embracing a more nuanced understanding of masculinity, individuals can break free from these constraints and cultivate a more inclusive and compassionate vision of what it means to be a man.

The journey of understanding male archetypes is a personal and transformative process, offering valuable insights and tools for personal growth and self-discovery. By exploring these archetypes, individuals can gain a deeper awareness of their own identities and the cultural narratives that shape their experiences. This exploration can foster personal growth, self-acceptance, and a more nuanced understanding of masculinity, ultimately leading to a more fulfilling and authentic life.

Overcoming Societal Expectations

Societal expectations are the invisible threads that weave through the fabric of our lives, shaping our beliefs, behaviors, and identities. These expectations, often rooted in cultural norms and traditions, dictate how individuals should think, act, and feel. While they can provide a sense of order and belonging, they can also impose limitations and stifle individuality. Overcoming societal expectations is a journey of self-discovery and empowerment, allowing individuals to break free from constraints and embrace their authentic selves.

The pressure to conform to societal expectations can manifest in various aspects of life, from career choices and relationships to personal appearance and lifestyle. These expectations are often communicated through family, peers, media, and institutions, creating a pervasive influence that can be difficult to resist. For many, the fear of judgment or rejection can lead to a reluctance to challenge these norms, resulting in a life that feels unfulfilling or inauthentic.

One of the first steps in overcoming societal expectations is cultivating self-awareness. By reflecting on personal values, desires, and goals, individuals can gain clarity on what truly matters to them, independent of external influences. This process of introspection involves questioning the beliefs and assumptions that have been internalized over time, identifying those that align with one's authentic self and those that do not. Journaling, meditation, and therapy can be valuable tools for fostering self-awareness and uncovering the motivations behind one's actions and decisions.

Once individuals have a clearer understanding of their authentic selves, they can begin to set boundaries and assert their autonomy. This involves communicating one's needs and desires to others, even when they conflict with societal expectations. Setting boundaries is an act of self-respect and empowerment, allowing individuals to prioritize their well-being and make choices that align with their values. While this process can be challenging, it is essential for cultivating a sense of agency and control over one's life.

Challenging societal expectations also requires the courage to embrace vulnerability and uncertainty. Stepping outside the confines of societal norms can evoke feelings of fear and insecurity, as individuals navigate uncharted territory and face potential criticism or rejection. However, embracing vulnerability is a powerful act of self-acceptance, allowing individuals to acknowledge their fears and insecurities without being defined by them. By cultivating resilience and self-compassion, individuals can navigate the challenges of breaking free from societal expectations with confidence and grace.

Building a supportive community is another crucial aspect of overcoming societal expectations. Surrounding oneself with like-minded individuals who share similar values and aspirations can provide encouragement and validation, reinforcing the belief that it is possible to live authentically. These connections can offer a sense of belonging and solidarity, reducing feelings of isolation and fostering a sense of empowerment. Engaging in communities, whether in person or online, can also provide opportunities for learning and growth, as individuals share experiences and insights with one another.

In addition to personal growth, overcoming societal expectations can have a broader impact on society as a whole. By challenging and redefining norms, individuals can contribute to a more inclusive and diverse culture that values individuality and authenticity. This process of cultural transformation involves questioning and dismantling systems of oppression and inequality, creating space for marginalized voices and perspectives. By embracing diversity and promoting acceptance, individuals can foster a more compassionate and equitable world.

The journey of overcoming societal expectations is not without its challenges, but it is a journey worth undertaking. By breaking free from the constraints of societal norms, individuals can cultivate a life that is true to their values and aspirations, leading to greater fulfillment and happiness. This journey is one of self-discovery and empowerment, offering valuable insights and tools for navigating the complexities of life with authenticity and resilience.

Ultimately, the process of overcoming societal expectations is a deeply personal and transformative experience. It requires courage, introspection, and a willingness to embrace uncertainty and change. By embarking on this journey, individuals can unlock their potential and live a life that is true to themselves, free from the limitations of societal norms. This journey is not only a path to personal growth and fulfillment but also a powerful act of resistance and empowerment, challenging the status quo and paving the way for a more inclusive and authentic world.

Building Confidence and Assertiveness

Confidence and assertiveness are essential qualities that empower individuals to express themselves authentically, pursue their goals, and navigate social interactions with ease. These traits are not innate but can be cultivated through intentional practice and self-reflection. By building confidence and assertiveness, individuals can enhance their self-esteem, improve their relationships, and achieve greater success in both personal and professional spheres.

Confidence is the belief in one's abilities and worth, providing a foundation for self-assurance and resilience. It is the inner voice that encourages individuals to take risks, embrace challenges, and trust in their capacity to succeed. Building confidence begins with self-awareness, an understanding of one's strengths and areas for growth. By acknowledging and celebrating achievements, individuals can reinforce their sense of competence and capability. This process involves setting realistic goals and breaking them down into manageable steps, allowing for incremental progress and the opportunity to experience success.

Positive self-talk is a powerful tool for building confidence, as it involves replacing negative or self-critical thoughts with affirming and supportive messages. By cultivating a mindset of self-compassion and encouragement, individuals can counteract self-doubt and foster a more positive self-image. Visualization techniques, such as imagining successful outcomes or rehearsing challenging situations, can also enhance confidence by mentally preparing individuals for real-life scenarios.

Assertiveness, on the other hand, is the ability to communicate one's needs, desires, and boundaries clearly and respectfully. It involves expressing oneself honestly while considering the perspectives and feelings of others. Assertiveness is not about being aggressive or domineering but rather about finding a balance between self-expression and empathy. By practicing assertiveness, individuals can build healthier and more equitable relationships, reducing misunderstandings and conflicts.

One of the key components of assertiveness is effective communication, which involves active listening, clear articulation, and nonverbal cues. Active listening requires giving full attention to the speaker, acknowledging their message, and responding thoughtfully. This practice fosters mutual understanding and respect, creating a supportive environment for open dialogue. Clear articulation involves expressing thoughts and feelings in a direct and concise manner, avoiding ambiguity or passive language. Nonverbal cues, such as eye contact, posture, and tone of voice, also play a crucial role in assertive communication, reinforcing the message being conveyed.

Setting boundaries is another important aspect of assertiveness, as it involves defining and communicating personal limits in various aspects of life. Boundaries are essential for maintaining self-respect and protecting one's well-being, as they prevent others from encroaching on one's time, energy, or values. By setting and enforcing boundaries, individuals can create a sense of autonomy and control, reducing stress and enhancing their quality of life.

Role-playing and practice are valuable strategies for developing assertiveness skills, as they provide opportunities to rehearse and refine communication techniques in a safe and supportive setting. By engaging in role-playing exercises, individuals can gain confidence in their ability to express themselves assertively and receive constructive feedback from others. This practice can also help individuals identify and address any underlying fears or anxieties that may hinder assertive behavior.

Building confidence and assertiveness is a gradual process that requires patience and persistence. It involves challenging limiting beliefs and stepping outside of one's comfort zone, embracing opportunities for growth and learning. By taking small, consistent steps toward self-improvement, individuals can gradually build their confidence and assertiveness, leading to greater empowerment and fulfillment.

The benefits of confidence and assertiveness extend beyond personal well-being, impacting professional success and leadership. Confident and assertive individuals are better equipped to advocate for themselves, negotiate effectively, and collaborate with others. These skills are highly valued in the workplace, as they contribute to a positive and productive work environment. By cultivating confidence and assertiveness, individuals can enhance their career prospects and contribute to the success of their organizations.

The journey of building confidence and assertiveness is one of self-discovery and empowerment, offering valuable insights and tools for navigating the complexities of life with authenticity and resilience. By embracing these qualities, individuals can enhance their well-being, improve their relationships, and achieve their goals. The development of confidence and assertiveness is a lifelong process, providing individuals with the foundation they need to thrive in an ever-changing world.

Navigating Emotional Vulnerability

Emotional vulnerability is a profound aspect of the human experience, often perceived as a double-edged sword. It is the state of being open to experiencing a wide range of emotions, from joy and love to fear and sadness. While vulnerability can evoke discomfort and fear of judgment, it is also a gateway to deeper connections, personal growth, and authentic living. Navigating emotional vulnerability requires courage, self-awareness, and a willingness to embrace the full spectrum of human emotions.

At its core, emotional vulnerability is about being honest with oneself and others about feelings and experiences. It involves acknowledging emotions without judgment and allowing oneself to be seen and heard. This openness can lead to more meaningful relationships, as it fosters trust and intimacy. When individuals share their vulnerabilities, they invite others to do the same, creating a space for mutual understanding and support.

The fear of vulnerability often stems from societal norms that equate emotional openness with weakness. Many individuals are conditioned to suppress or hide their emotions, fearing rejection or ridicule. However, vulnerability is not a sign of weakness; it is a testament to one's strength and authenticity. By embracing vulnerability, individuals can break free from the constraints of societal expectations and cultivate a more genuine and fulfilling life.

One of the first steps in navigating emotional vulnerability is developing self-awareness. This involves recognizing and understanding one's emotions, triggers, and patterns of behavior. By cultivating self-awareness, individuals can gain insight into their emotional landscape and identify areas for growth and healing. Journaling, meditation, and therapy are valuable tools for fostering self-awareness and exploring the depths of one's emotions.

Once individuals have a clearer understanding of their emotions, they can begin to practice self-compassion. This involves treating oneself with kindness and understanding, especially during moments of vulnerability. Self-compassion allows individuals to acknowledge their emotions without judgment, creating a safe space for healing and growth. By embracing self-compassion, individuals can build resilience and reduce the fear of vulnerability.

Communicating vulnerability to others is another important aspect of navigating emotional openness. This involves expressing emotions honestly and openly, while also being mindful of the impact on others. Effective communication requires active listening, empathy, and a willingness to engage in open dialogue. By sharing vulnerabilities with trusted individuals, individuals can build stronger and more supportive relationships, enhancing their sense of connection and belonging.

Setting boundaries is also crucial for navigating emotional vulnerability. Boundaries are essential for protecting one's emotional well-being and ensuring that vulnerability is shared in a safe and respectful manner. By setting and communicating boundaries, individuals can create a sense of autonomy and control, reducing the risk of emotional harm. Boundaries also allow individuals to prioritize their needs and well-being, fostering a sense of empowerment and self-respect.

The journey of navigating emotional vulnerability is not without its challenges, but it is a journey worth undertaking. By embracing vulnerability, individuals can unlock their potential for personal growth and transformation. This process involves stepping outside of one's comfort zone and embracing the unknown, with the understanding that vulnerability is a natural and essential part of the human experience.

The benefits of embracing emotional vulnerability extend beyond personal well-being, impacting relationships and social interactions. Vulnerable individuals are better equipped to form deep and meaningful connections, as they are willing to share their true selves with others. This openness fosters trust and intimacy, creating a supportive environment for mutual growth and understanding. By cultivating vulnerability, individuals can enhance their relationships and contribute to a more compassionate and empathetic world.

The journey of navigating emotional vulnerability is one of self-discovery and empowerment, offering valuable insights and tools for living authentically and resiliently. By embracing vulnerability, individuals can enhance their well-being, improve their relationships, and achieve their goals. The development of emotional vulnerability is a lifelong process, providing individuals with the foundation they need to thrive in an ever-changing world.

Cultivating Leadership and Influence

Leadership and influence are pivotal forces that shape the dynamics of communities, organizations, and societies. They are not confined to positions of authority but are qualities that can be cultivated by anyone willing to inspire, guide, and impact others positively. Cultivating leadership and influence involves developing a set of skills and attributes that empower individuals to motivate and lead by example, fostering environments where collaboration and innovation thrive.

At the heart of effective leadership is the ability to communicate a clear and compelling vision. A leader's vision serves as a guiding star, providing direction and purpose for both the leader and their followers. This vision must be communicated with clarity and passion, inspiring others to share in the journey toward a common goal. Storytelling is a powerful tool in this regard, as it allows leaders to convey their vision in a relatable and engaging manner, connecting with the emotions and aspirations of their audience.

Empathy is another cornerstone of leadership, enabling leaders to understand and connect with the needs and perspectives of others. By cultivating empathy, leaders can build trust and rapport, creating a supportive environment where individuals feel valued and heard. This involves active listening, being present in conversations, and demonstrating genuine concern for the well-being of others. Empathetic leaders are adept at navigating interpersonal dynamics, resolving conflicts, and fostering a sense of community and belonging.

Decision-making is a critical aspect of leadership, requiring the ability to assess situations, weigh options, and make informed choices. Effective leaders are decisive yet flexible, able to adapt to changing circumstances and incorporate new information. This involves a balance of analytical thinking and intuition, as well as the courage to take calculated risks. By involving others in the decision-making process, leaders can leverage diverse perspectives and expertise, enhancing the quality and acceptance of their decisions.

Influence, closely tied to leadership, is the capacity to affect the attitudes and behaviors of others. It is not about exerting control or authority but rather about inspiring and motivating others to take action. Influential leaders lead by example, embodying the values and principles they wish to instill in others. This authenticity and integrity are key to building credibility and trust, which are essential for effective influence.

Building a strong network is vital for cultivating influence, as it provides access to resources, information, and support. Networking involves establishing and nurturing relationships with individuals across various fields and backgrounds, creating a web of connections that can be leveraged for mutual benefit.

By engaging with diverse perspectives and experiences, leaders can broaden their understanding and enhance their ability to influence others.

Mentorship is a powerful avenue for developing leadership and influence, offering opportunities for learning and growth through guidance and support. By seeking out mentors, individuals can gain valuable insights and advice from those with experience and expertise. Conversely, by serving as mentors, individuals can share their knowledge and skills, fostering the development of future leaders and expanding their influence.

Self-awareness is a fundamental component of leadership, involving an understanding of one's strengths, weaknesses, and impact on others. By cultivating self-awareness, leaders can identify areas for growth and development, enhancing their effectiveness and adaptability. This involves regular reflection and feedback, as well as a commitment to continuous learning and improvement.

Resilience is another essential quality for leaders, enabling them to navigate challenges and setbacks with perseverance and determination. Resilient leaders maintain a positive outlook, viewing obstacles as opportunities for growth and innovation. By fostering a culture of resilience, leaders can inspire others to embrace change and uncertainty with confidence and creativity.

The journey of cultivating leadership and influence is one of self-discovery and transformation, offering valuable insights and tools for making a meaningful impact in the world. By embracing these qualities, individuals can enhance their ability to inspire and guide others, contributing to the success and well-being of their communities and organizations. Leadership and influence are not static traits but dynamic processes that evolve with experience and reflection, providing individuals with the foundation they need to thrive in an ever-changing world.

Breaking Free from Gender Stereotypes

Gender stereotypes are deeply ingrained societal constructs that dictate how individuals should behave, think, and feel based on their gender. These stereotypes often limit personal expression and potential, confining individuals to rigid roles and expectations. Breaking free from gender stereotypes is a journey of self-discovery and liberation, allowing individuals to embrace their authentic selves and contribute to a more inclusive and equitable society.

From a young age, individuals are exposed to gender stereotypes through various channels, including family, media, education, and peer interactions. These stereotypes often manifest in the form of expectations about appearance, behavior, interests, and career choices. For example, traditional stereotypes may dictate that men should be strong, assertive, and unemotional, while women should be nurturing, passive, and sensitive. Such stereotypes not only restrict individual expression but also perpetuate inequality and discrimination.

The first step in breaking free from gender stereotypes is developing self-awareness and critical thinking. This involves questioning and challenging the beliefs and assumptions that have been internalized over time. By reflecting on personal values, desires, and goals, individuals can gain clarity on what truly matters to them, independent of societal expectations.

This process of introspection allows individuals to identify and dismantle the stereotypes that have influenced their self-perception and behavior.

Education and exposure to diverse perspectives are powerful tools for challenging gender stereotypes. By learning about different cultures, histories, and experiences, individuals can broaden their understanding of gender and recognize the fluidity and diversity of human identity. Engaging with literature, art, and media that challenge traditional gender norms can also provide inspiration and validation for those seeking to break free from stereotypes.

Building a supportive community is essential for fostering an environment where individuals feel empowered to express themselves authentically. Surrounding oneself with like-minded individuals who share similar values and aspirations can provide encouragement and validation, reinforcing the belief that it is possible to live authentically. These connections can offer a sense of belonging and solidarity, reducing feelings of isolation and fostering a sense of empowerment.

Advocacy and activism play a crucial role in challenging and dismantling gender stereotypes on a broader scale. By raising awareness and promoting dialogue about gender equality, individuals can contribute to cultural transformation and social change. This involves speaking out against discrimination and inequality, supporting policies and initiatives that promote inclusivity, and amplifying the voices of marginalized communities. Through collective action, individuals can create a more equitable and just society that values diversity and individuality.

Role models and mentors can provide guidance and inspiration for those seeking to break free from gender stereotypes. By observing and learning from individuals who have successfully navigated the challenges of defying societal norms, individuals can gain valuable insights and strategies for their own journey. Mentorship offers opportunities for learning and growth through guidance and support, fostering the development of future leaders and change-makers.

Self-compassion and resilience are essential qualities for navigating the challenges of breaking free from gender stereotypes. This involves treating oneself with kindness and understanding, especially during moments of vulnerability and uncertainty. By cultivating self-compassion, individuals can build resilience and reduce the fear of judgment or rejection. Resilient individuals maintain a positive outlook, viewing obstacles as opportunities for growth and innovation.

The journey of breaking free from gender stereotypes is not without its challenges, but it is a journey worth undertaking. By embracing individuality and authenticity, individuals can unlock their potential for personal growth and transformation. This process involves stepping outside of one's comfort zone and embracing the unknown, with the understanding that gender is a natural and essential part of the human experience.

The benefits of breaking free from gender stereotypes extend beyond personal well-being, impacting relationships and social interactions. Individuals who embrace their authentic selves are better equipped to form deep and meaningful connections, as they are willing to share their true selves with others. This openness fosters trust and intimacy, creating a supportive environment for mutual growth and understanding. By challenging gender stereotypes, individuals can enhance their relationships and contribute to a more compassionate and empathetic world.

Ultimately, the process of breaking free from gender stereotypes is a deeply personal and transformative experience. It requires courage, introspection, and a willingness to embrace uncertainty and change. By embarking on this journey, individuals can unlock their potential and live a life that is true to themselves, free from the limitations of societal norms. This journey is not only a path to personal growth and fulfillment but also a powerful act of resistance and empowerment, challenging the status quo and paving the way for a more inclusive and authentic world.

Harnessing Feminine Strengths

Feminine strengths, often undervalued in traditional societal frameworks, encompass a range of qualities that can be harnessed to foster personal growth, leadership, and community building. These strengths, which include empathy, intuition, collaboration, and nurturing, are not exclusive to any gender but are often associated with feminine energy. By recognizing and embracing these strengths, individuals can unlock their potential and contribute to a more balanced and harmonious world.

Empathy, the ability to understand and share the feelings of others, is a powerful tool for building connections and fostering understanding. It allows individuals to see the world from different perspectives, creating a foundation for compassion and cooperation. In leadership, empathy enables individuals to connect with their team members on a deeper level, understanding their needs and motivations. This connection fosters a supportive and inclusive environment where individuals feel valued and heard, leading to increased morale and productivity.

Intuition, often described as a gut feeling or inner knowing, is another valuable feminine strength. It involves tapping into one's subconscious mind to make decisions and solve problems. Intuition can guide individuals in navigating complex situations, providing insights that may not be immediately apparent through logical reasoning alone. By trusting their intuition, individuals can make more informed and confident decisions, enhancing their ability to lead and innovate.

Collaboration is a hallmark of feminine strengths, emphasizing the importance of working together to achieve common goals. Collaborative individuals prioritize teamwork and cooperation, recognizing that diverse perspectives and skills can lead to more creative and effective solutions. In a collaborative environment, individuals are encouraged to share their ideas and contribute to the collective success of the group. This approach fosters a sense of community and belonging, empowering individuals to take ownership of their work and contribute to the greater good.

Nurturing, the ability to care for and support others, is a strength that can be harnessed to build strong and resilient communities. Nurturing individuals create environments where others feel safe and supported, fostering growth and development. In leadership, nurturing involves mentoring and guiding others, helping them to reach their full potential. This approach not only benefits individuals but also strengthens the organization as a whole, creating a culture of continuous learning and improvement.

To harness feminine strengths, individuals must first recognize and value these qualities within themselves and others. This involves challenging societal norms that may devalue or dismiss feminine strengths, embracing a more inclusive and holistic understanding of leadership and success. By celebrating and cultivating these strengths, individuals can create a more balanced and equitable world where diverse talents and perspectives are valued and utilized.

Developing self-awareness is a crucial step in harnessing feminine strengths. This involves reflecting on one's values, beliefs, and behaviors, identifying areas for growth and development. By cultivating self-awareness, individuals can gain a deeper understanding of their strengths and how to leverage them effectively. This process may involve seeking feedback from others, engaging in self-reflection, and exploring new experiences and opportunities for growth.

Mentorship and role models can provide valuable guidance and inspiration for those seeking to harness feminine strengths. By observing and learning from individuals who embody these qualities, individuals can gain insights and strategies for their own journey. Mentorship offers opportunities for learning and growth through guidance and support, fostering the development of future leaders and change-makers.

Creating supportive environments is essential for nurturing feminine strengths. This involves fostering a culture of inclusivity and respect, where diverse perspectives and talents are valued and encouraged. By creating spaces where individuals feel safe to express themselves and share their ideas, organizations can harness the full potential of their members, leading to greater innovation and success.

The journey of harnessing feminine strengths is one of self-discovery and empowerment, offering valuable insights and tools for living authentically and resiliently. By embracing these qualities, individuals can enhance their well-being, improve their relationships, and achieve their goals. The development of feminine strengths is a lifelong process, providing individuals with the foundation they need to thrive in an ever-changing world.

Ultimately, harnessing feminine strengths is about embracing a more inclusive and holistic understanding of leadership and success. By recognizing and valuing these qualities, individuals can contribute to a more balanced and harmonious world, where diverse talents and perspectives are celebrated and utilized. This journey is not only a path to personal growth and fulfillment but also a powerful act of resistance and empowerment, challenging the status quo and paving the way for a more inclusive and authentic world.

Building a Supportive Network

A supportive network is an invaluable asset in both personal and professional realms, providing encouragement, resources, and opportunities for growth. Building such a network involves cultivating relationships with individuals who share similar values, interests, and goals, as well as those who offer diverse perspectives and expertise. A well-rounded network can enhance one's ability to navigate challenges, seize opportunities, and achieve success.

The foundation of a supportive network lies in genuine connections, which are built on trust, respect, and mutual benefit. To establish these connections, it is essential to approach networking with authenticity and openness. This means being true to oneself, expressing genuine interest in others, and being willing to share one's own experiences and insights. Authentic connections are more likely to endure and provide meaningful support over time.

One effective way to build a supportive network is through active participation in communities and organizations that align with one's interests and goals. This could include professional associations, volunteer groups, social clubs, or online forums. By engaging with these communities, individuals can meet like-minded people, exchange ideas, and collaborate on projects. Participation in such groups also provides opportunities to develop new skills and gain valuable insights from others.

Networking events, whether in-person or virtual, offer additional opportunities to expand one's network. These events provide a platform for meeting new people, learning about different industries and fields, and sharing one's own expertise. To make the most of networking events, it is important to approach them with a clear purpose and an open mind. This involves setting specific goals, such as meeting a certain number of new contacts or learning about a particular topic, and being open to unexpected opportunities and connections.

Building a supportive network also involves nurturing existing relationships. This means maintaining regular communication, offering support and assistance, and expressing appreciation for the contributions of others. By investing time and effort into maintaining relationships, individuals can strengthen their network and ensure that it remains a valuable source of support and collaboration.

Mentorship is a key component of a supportive network, offering guidance, advice, and encouragement from those with more experience or expertise. Seeking out mentors can provide valuable insights and perspectives, helping individuals navigate challenges and make informed decisions. Conversely, serving as a mentor to others can be a rewarding experience, offering opportunities to share knowledge and contribute to the development of future leaders.

Diversity is an important consideration when building a supportive network. A diverse network includes individuals from different backgrounds, industries, and areas of expertise, providing a wide range of perspectives and insights. By embracing diversity, individuals can enhance their ability to innovate, solve problems, and adapt to changing circumstances. A diverse network also fosters inclusivity and empathy, creating a more supportive and collaborative environment.

Reciprocity is a fundamental principle of a supportive network, emphasizing the importance of giving as well as receiving. This means being willing to offer assistance, share resources, and provide support to others, without expecting anything in return. By fostering a culture of reciprocity, individuals can build stronger and more resilient networks, where members are motivated to support and uplift one another.

Technology plays a significant role in building and maintaining a supportive network, offering tools and platforms for communication, collaboration, and connection. Social media, professional networking sites, and online communities provide opportunities to connect with individuals across the globe, expanding the reach and diversity of one's network. By leveraging technology, individuals can stay connected with their network, share information and resources, and collaborate on projects, regardless of geographical location.

The journey of building a supportive network is one of continuous growth and evolution, offering valuable insights and opportunities for personal and professional development. By embracing authenticity, diversity, and reciprocity, individuals can create a network that supports their goals and aspirations, while also contributing to the success and well-being of others. A supportive network is not only a source of encouragement and resources but also a powerful catalyst for innovation, collaboration, and positive change.

Balancing Ambition and Empathy

Balancing ambition and empathy is a nuanced art that requires a delicate equilibrium between pursuing personal goals and understanding the needs and emotions of others. In a world that often glorifies relentless ambition, empathy can sometimes be overshadowed, yet it remains an essential component of meaningful success and fulfillment. By integrating empathy into one's ambitious pursuits, individuals can create a more harmonious and impactful journey, benefiting both themselves and those around them.

Ambition is the driving force that propels individuals toward their goals, fueling determination, resilience, and innovation. It is the spark that ignites passion and motivates individuals to push beyond their limits, striving for excellence and achievement. However, unchecked ambition can lead to a narrow focus on personal success, potentially resulting in burnout, strained relationships, and ethical compromises. To harness the full potential of ambition, it is crucial to temper it with empathy, ensuring that one's pursuits are aligned with values and contribute positively to the broader community.

Empathy, the ability to understand and share the feelings of others, serves as a compass that guides individuals in their interactions and decisions. It fosters connection, trust, and collaboration, creating an environment where individuals feel valued and supported. By cultivating empathy, individuals can gain a deeper understanding of the impact of their actions on others, allowing them to make more informed and compassionate choices. This awareness can enhance leadership, improve relationships, and contribute to a more inclusive and equitable society.

The integration of ambition and empathy begins with self-awareness, a critical component of personal growth and development. Self-awareness involves reflecting on one's values, motivations, and behaviors, identifying areas for growth and alignment. By understanding the driving forces behind their ambition, individuals can ensure that their goals are in harmony with their values and contribute to the well-being of others. This process of introspection allows individuals to identify potential blind spots and biases, fostering a more empathetic and balanced approach to their pursuits.

Effective communication is another key element in balancing ambition and empathy. This involves actively listening to others, seeking to understand their perspectives and needs, and expressing one's own thoughts and feelings with clarity and respect. By engaging in open and honest dialogue, individuals can build trust and rapport, creating a supportive environment where collaboration and innovation thrive. Communication also provides opportunities to address conflicts and misunderstandings, ensuring that ambition does not overshadow empathy in interactions and relationships.

Collaboration is a powerful way to integrate ambition and empathy, emphasizing the importance of working together to achieve common goals. Collaborative individuals recognize that diverse perspectives and skills can lead to more creative and effective solutions, enhancing the quality and impact of their work. By fostering a culture of collaboration, individuals can harness the strengths of their team members, creating a sense of shared purpose and mutual support. This approach not only enhances individual success but also contributes to the success and well-being of the collective.

Setting boundaries is essential for maintaining a healthy balance between ambition and empathy. Boundaries provide a framework for prioritizing one's needs and well-being, ensuring that ambition does not come at the expense of personal health or relationships. By setting and communicating boundaries, individuals can create a sense of autonomy and control, reducing the risk of burnout and emotional exhaustion. Boundaries also allow individuals to allocate time and energy to nurturing relationships and practicing self-care, fostering a more sustainable and fulfilling journey.

Mentorship and role models can provide valuable guidance and inspiration for those seeking to balance ambition and empathy.

By observing and learning from individuals who embody these qualities, individuals can gain insights and strategies for their own journey. Mentorship offers opportunities for learning and growth through guidance and support, fostering the development of future leaders and change-makers who prioritize both ambition and empathy in their pursuits.

Resilience is another essential quality for navigating the challenges of balancing ambition and empathy. Resilient individuals maintain a positive outlook, viewing obstacles as opportunities for growth and innovation. By cultivating resilience, individuals can navigate setbacks and challenges with perseverance and determination, ensuring that empathy remains a guiding force in their journey. Resilience also fosters adaptability and flexibility, allowing individuals to adjust their approach and priorities as needed, maintaining a healthy balance between ambition and empathy.

The journey of balancing ambition and empathy is one of continuous growth and evolution, offering valuable insights and opportunities for personal and professional development. By embracing these qualities, individuals can enhance their well-being, improve their relationships, and achieve their goals in a way that is aligned with their values and contributes positively to the broader community. Balancing ambition and empathy is not only a path to personal growth and fulfillment but also a powerful act of resistance and empowerment, challenging the status quo and paving the way for a more inclusive and authentic world.

Strategies for Effective Communication

Effective communication is the cornerstone of successful relationships, both personal and professional. It is the bridge that connects individuals, allowing them to share ideas, express emotions, and collaborate toward common goals. Mastering the art of communication involves more than just exchanging words; it requires understanding, empathy, and the ability to convey messages clearly and persuasively. By employing a range of strategies, individuals can enhance their communication skills and foster more meaningful connections.

Active listening is a fundamental component of effective communication. It involves fully engaging with the speaker, paying attention to their words, tone, and body language, and responding thoughtfully. Active listening demonstrates respect and interest, creating a supportive environment where individuals feel valued and understood. To practice active listening, it is important to maintain eye contact, nod or provide verbal affirmations, and avoid interrupting or formulating responses while the other person is speaking. By focusing on the speaker's message, individuals can gain a deeper understanding of their perspective and respond more effectively.

Clarity and conciseness are essential for conveying messages effectively. Clear communication involves expressing thoughts and ideas in a straightforward and unambiguous manner, avoiding jargon or overly complex language. Conciseness ensures that the message is delivered efficiently, without unnecessary details or repetition. To achieve clarity and conciseness, it is helpful to organize thoughts before speaking, use simple and direct language, and focus on the key points. This approach not only enhances understanding but also reduces the likelihood of misunderstandings or confusion.

Nonverbal communication plays a significant role in conveying messages and emotions. Body language, facial expressions, gestures, and tone of voice all contribute to the overall message and can either reinforce or contradict verbal communication. Being aware of one's own nonverbal cues and interpreting those of others can enhance communication and build rapport. For example, maintaining an open posture, using appropriate gestures, and modulating tone can convey confidence and sincerity, while avoiding crossed arms or averted gaze can prevent the perception of defensiveness or disinterest.

Empathy is a powerful tool for effective communication, allowing individuals to connect with others on an emotional level. By putting oneself in another's shoes, individuals can better understand their feelings and perspectives, fostering a sense of connection and trust. Empathetic communication involves acknowledging and validating the emotions of others, expressing understanding and support, and being sensitive to their needs and concerns. This approach not only strengthens relationships but also facilitates collaboration and conflict resolution.

Feedback is an important aspect of communication, providing opportunities for growth and improvement. Constructive feedback involves offering specific, actionable, and respectful suggestions for improvement, while also acknowledging strengths and achievements. When giving feedback, it is important to focus on behaviors rather than personal attributes, use "I" statements to express one's perspective, and provide examples to illustrate points. Receiving feedback with an open mind and a willingness to learn can also enhance communication skills and foster personal development.

Adaptability is a key strategy for effective communication, as it involves adjusting one's approach based on the context, audience, and purpose of the interaction. This may involve varying the level of formality, tone, or language to suit different situations or individuals. For example, communicating with a colleague may require a different approach than communicating with a friend or family member. By being adaptable, individuals can ensure that their message is received and understood, regardless of the circumstances.

Storytelling is a powerful communication technique that can engage, inspire, and persuade audiences. By weaving narratives into communication, individuals can convey complex ideas in a relatable and memorable way. Storytelling involves using vivid language, relatable characters, and compelling plots to capture the audience's attention and evoke emotions. This approach can be particularly effective in presentations, negotiations, or any situation where persuasion or motivation is desired.

Conflict resolution is an important aspect of communication, as it involves addressing and resolving disagreements or misunderstandings in a constructive manner. Effective conflict resolution requires active listening, empathy, and a focus on finding mutually beneficial solutions. This may involve identifying common goals, exploring different perspectives, and negotiating compromises. By approaching conflicts with a collaborative mindset, individuals can strengthen relationships and prevent future misunderstandings.

Confidence is a crucial element of effective communication, as it influences how messages are perceived and received. Confident communicators convey authority and credibility, making it more likely that their message will be taken seriously and respected. Building confidence in communication involves practicing and refining skills, preparing thoroughly for interactions, and maintaining a positive mindset. By projecting confidence, individuals can enhance their ability to persuade and influence others.

The journey of mastering effective communication is one of continuous learning and growth, offering valuable insights and opportunities for personal and professional development. By employing these strategies, individuals can enhance their ability to connect with others, convey their message clearly, and achieve their goals. Effective communication is not only a path to personal success and fulfillment but also a powerful tool for building stronger, more collaborative, and more empathetic communities.